venice

AND ITS TREASURES

422 COLOUR ILLUSTRATIONS

VENICE

CITY AND LAGOON
an indissoluble and vital synthesis

During the long course of a historical process that had begun when the Roman Empire showed the first signs of an impending decadence, the Tenth Region, that is *Venetia et Histria*, was one of the areas most tortured.

Life within the region became ever more precarious as the years went by. The population learned to its cost the wisdom of abandoning property, dragging away what goods they could, to seek refuge in the Lagoon isles.

In 584 when the Eastern Empire, bent on conquering a part of the Italian territory, established the Exarchate of Ravenna, the lagoon community passed under the direct sovereignty of Byzantium.

Later events, however, were to reduce this sovereignty to a mere formality.

The end of the Exarchate of Ravenna in 751 coincided with the transfer of the seat of government from Cittanova Eracliana to Malamocco: at this moment the mainland party, supporters of the Franks, gathered their forces together.

Finally, with the election of Doge Angelo Partecipazio, the Byzantine party prevailed. The Doge declared himself dependent upon Byzantium, realizing that the distance separating Venice from the centre of the Eastern Empire would rob of its content this dependence which could more than anything else protect the community « de jure » from the expansionist policy of the Franks.

Heading towards the Chioggia lagoon from the mainland, the Franks, who had taken the place of the Lombards, endeavoured to subjugate the Venetians and under Pippin, son of Charlemagne (809), the threat to their liberty was so great that the hatred between various islands quietened down.

Two decisions taken at that time proved fundamental in the future development of the city. The political centre was shifted to Rivus Altus, the most protected part of the lagoon; in 829 two merchants from Alexandria in Egypt brought the body of St. Mark to Rialto where it superseded the Greek St. Theodore as protector of the new city.

3

WATER, " BARENE," " GHEBI," SILENCE AND SOLITUDE. A NATURAL ENVIRONMENT LEFT UNALTERED FOR CENTURIES

4

Thus the Venetians wanted freedom and independence also from Byzantium.

The city of Venice, therefore, rose upon the islands of Rivoaltus in the year 810, when a group of men, at the head of whom was Angelo Partecipazio, decided to abandon Malamocco, at that time the most important centre, and to move over to these new islands in the middle of the lagoon. Only then did Venice come to birth, not only materially but spiritually as well.

The new generations, for whom the environment of the lagoon provided the setting for every human activity, thought of their existence in terms of this environment, and of the advantages which, without any doubt, were connected with it. On these little islands they created new centres of power and riches, autonomous and at the same time safe.

THE FIRST POLITICAL-SOCIAL TOWNS ON THE LAGOON

Towards the southern extremity of the island is to be found the ancient centre of Malamocco, known in olden times by the name of Matamaucus, where in 742 was established the seat of government, formerly at Heraclea, and here it remained until 810 when it passed to Rivoaltus or Rialto.

The ancient Malamocco seems to have been completely destroyed by a great upheaval of the sea in 1107, and rebuilt a few years later, farther back.

From charts and documents of 1150 onwards, the community became known as Malamocco Novo. It enjoyed special privileges, and it also had its own Podestà.

In the little square where stands the Church, there is still the Gothic style building of the Podestà.

GRADO CITTANOVA MALAMOCCO

5

2   The Venetian lagoon
3   Sandy shore on the sea side
4   Fishing huts, J. de Barbari
5   Malamocco

3

RIVOALTO
ANGELO PARTECIPAZIO

A NEW CITY WAS BORN
IN THE YEAR 810

VENICE

The 8th Century saw the slow development of a new policy in a territory that had already, in the two preceding centuries, been defining itself more and more clearly, not merely geographically on account of its particular natural situation, but also as the permanent seat of a population in pursuit of an internal organization of its own.

These successive phases of achievement extended from the initial search for the necessary means of survival right up to the more or less organic structure of ordinances for a community that by now had become numerous. Cittanova, Torcello, Malamocco and last, but by no means least Rivoaltus, were the principal seats of the earliest political, social and commercial organizations. With the decision arrived at in 810 to transfer the seat of government to the islands of Rialto, was embodied the wish to be freed from an entire series of relations and dependence, often at odds with each other, which had hindered any discourse of a united character that might have been to the advantage of the new community.

With this precise intention, the new city came to birth and grew to maturity, but even before the city itself, came the establishment of the two most significant centres round which developed the building fabric, St. Mark's Square and the Rialto market.

The chosen ambient was safe but not easy; life at first was difficult and uncomfortable. Poor, miserable, little maritime villages began to spring up; huts resting on poles, high above the water and sandbanks, ground floor dwellings with walls of stone brought by the Venetians from the mainland together with other merchandise, the fruits of their trading and exchange undertakings. The flat-bottomed boat became an element of prime importance in the life of the lagoon dwellers, and the most ideal means of maintaining relations with the mainland.

Cassiodorus, counsellor to King Theodoric (6th Century) writes thus about the lagoon landscape: « Down there are lagoon houses almost like waterfowls' nests now terrestrial now insular and when there is a change in the appearance of the place, suddenly they resemble the Cyclades, those widely scattered dwellings, made not by nature, but by the industry of man » and « ...the boats that you keep tied to your walls, like animals ».

The inhabitants of the lagoon, the nobles and the common people, had organized themselves right from the very beginning, making the most of the natural resources of the territory (salt, fish) and weaving a network of advantageous commercial relationships, leaving out of consideration political situations, which they avoided so as to keep their various undertakings active in all circumstances.

Already in the 7th Century, and from then onwards, the Venetian merchants were thrusting forward with their ships as far as the coast of Africa.

They could reach Rome by land or by sea, going up the Tyrrhenian Sea. An enormous amount of traffic developed in the ports of the Adriatic and along the waterways leading to the Italian interior.

If at first private and personal initiative had been sufficient, even a determining factor, it is clear that later on the increase in the volume of business, in the number of lines of communication, and in the tonnage of the vessels, called for a more complex organization, a true and proper form of government.

More and more often officialdom was called for in relations with other nations or states; a more stable backing was necessary nowadays in the conquest of new markets and in the establishment of commercial bases which would facilitate the business of exchange.

By allying themselves with the Byzantines, the Venetians won a series of naval victories against the pirates of Dalmatia, the Saracens and the Normans; and while on the one hand they obtained privileges, on the other they imposed their own authority along the coasts of the Adriatic.

So far as concerned the population of the mainland, Venice limited herself to maintaining commercial relations and, to facilitate these, drew up agreements about landing and transit.

Salt proved to be her most valuable asset in smoothing out difficulties, it was her most precious commercial asset. The Crusades found the cities of Pisa, Genoa and Venice ready to seize upon all possible commercial advantages that might derive from transport and exchange.

At the beginning Venice, eager not to jeopardize the privileged position she enjoyed in the Byzantine ports, had held off, but once she realized the wonderful benefits all this was bringing to her rivals, threw herself into the fray and succeeded in concluding the formidable enterprise of the IV Crusade, as a result of which she became the mistress of « one quarter and a half of the Empire of Constantinople ».

The European heads of government, nobles and princes proposed the Imperial Purple to the Doge Enrico Dandolo who had led the expedition. But the elderly Doge was immune to flattery and contented himself with the possession of certain commercial bases and quite a number of the islands of the Aegean Sea, Methoni and Koroni, in addition to Crete. On this occasion we see the continuance of the line of policy chosen in preceding centuries, no annexation of territories, costly and difficult to control, but efficient naval bases in all Mediterranean ports.

THE ADRIATIC AND THE MEDITERRANEAN
navigation routes

7

8

the bases of a stable government are established and the policies for the development of a commercial empire decided

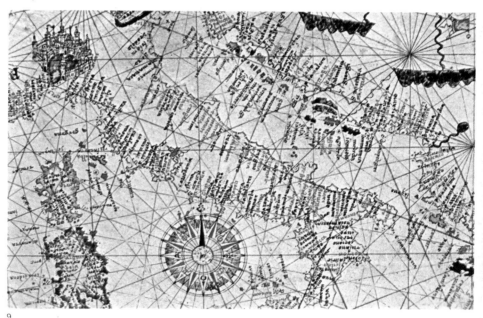

9

VENICE AND CONSTANTINOPLE

11

12

ISLANDS AND SHORES

MURANO
BURANO
TORCELLO
SAN FRANCESCO DEL
        DESERTO
SAN LAZZARO
LE VIGNOLE
LIDO
MALAMOCCO
PELLESTRINA
CHIOGGIA

13

BURANO
lace and fish

Burano announces its presence from far away on the flat, pale profile of the lagoon, with the bright colours of its low buildings and its tall, leaning bell-tower.
A visit to the island is well worth while, not just because of the importance of its architectural elements but also for a glimpse into the life of this fishing community where the centuries-old dialogue between man and the sea still goes on, and again for the building network that has to a great extent been preserved, if not in the actual original buildings, in the type of low houses, poor but brightly coloured. The lace of Burano, too, is as celebrated as the fine glass of Murano.

14

Close to Torcello, the little island of S. Francesco del Deserto, with the evocative green of its tall cypresses, makes one think of the one-time natural configuration which must have been that of similar places in the lagoon, now transformed.
The fame of this island is due to the coming of St. Francis who moored there in 1220 on his return from Syria, while a fierce storm raged. On the opposite part of Burano, facing S. Francesco del Deserto, are the islands of Sant'Erasmo and the Vignole, devoted to vegetable gardens and vineyards.

SAN FRANCESCO DEL DESERTO

6

15

A VERY OLD CATHEDRAL AT TORCELLO

16

Even as one draws near to the island of Torcello one is overcome by the fascination of this strange place, so isolated in the lagoon, where the remains of the oldest lagoon civilization still stand. Torcello was the seat of a commercial centre of considerable importance.
The physical changes in the environment, the silting up of the rivers and the formation of swampy, boggy areas, together with the complete disappearance of some tiny islands, for reasons not very clear, led fairly quickly to the decay and abandonment of this archipelago for other shores.
Certain religious buildings, the only ones preserved, still remain, mute testimony of past splendour: the Church of Santa Maria Genitrice, and that of Santa Fosca.
The remains of a stone plaque, dated 639 confirm the hypothesis of the earliest erection of the Church of Santa Maria Genitrice. Towards the end of the 7th Century work proceeded on the first reconstruction.
Of this fabric only the lower part of the apse remains to-day. In 864 there was a second reconstruction; the building was greatly enlarged, both longitudinally, as far as the ancient Baptistery, of which only the foundations remain, and also transversely, with the addition of the lateral naves.
The last radical restoration, during which the columns and capitals of the central nave were renewed, together with the open-beamed wooden ceiling and the mosaic floor, dates back to 1008, that is to say when Orso, son of the Doge Pietro Orseolo II, rose to the position of Bishop of Torcello.

The porch on the façade was renewed at the end of the 14th Century. The lateral windows are interesting for the fact that they have shutters made of slabs of stone.
The bowl of the central apse and the triumphal arch are covered with mosaics, representing on high « The Virgin Mother of God » and lower down « The Twelve Apostles », and on the arch « The Annunciation ». Even if the iconography belongs to the 7th Century, the execution of these mosaics, though it is difficult to assign a precise date, might well go back to the 12th Century.
On the internal wall of the façade, above the entrance door, is a huge mosaic depicting « The Apotheosis of Christ and the Last Judgment ». The bell-tower belongs to the last period of the works (1008).
Santa Fosca, built a first time, it would seem, in 864, to a basilical plan, was re-built in the 10th Century to a central plan.

17

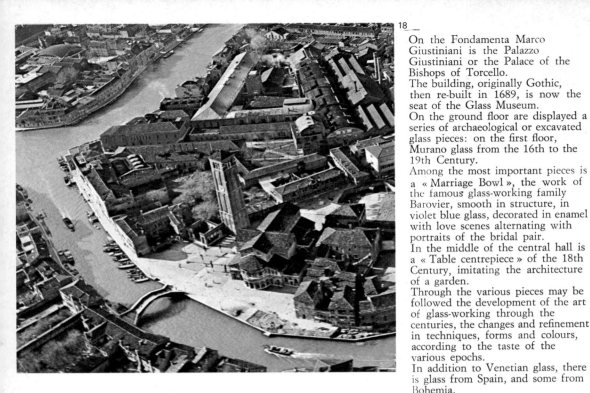

On the Fondamenta Marco Giustiniani is the Palazzo Giustiniani or the Palace of the Bishops of Torcello.

The building, originally Gothic, then re-built in 1689, is now the seat of the Glass Museum.

On the ground floor are displayed a series of archaeological or excavated glass pieces: on the first floor, Murano glass from the 16th to the 19th Century.

Among the most important pieces is a « Marriage Bowl », the work of the famous glass-working family Barovier, smooth in structure, in violet blue glass, decorated in enamel with love scenes alternating with portraits of the bridal pair.

In the middle of the central hall is a « Table centrepiece » of the 18th Century, imitating the architecture of a garden.

Through the various pieces may be followed the development of the art of glass-working through the centuries, the changes and refinement in techniques, forms and colours, according to the taste of the various epochs.

In addition to Venetian glass, there is glass from Spain, and some from Bohemia.

MURANO GLASS KNOWN AND ESTEEMED IN ALL EUROPE

The island of Murano, like other islands of this part of the lagoon, seat of refugees fleeing the mainland under the onrush of the barbaric invasions, first developed basing its economy on Torcello, then on Venice from the beginning of the 9th Century and onwards.

It enjoyed a certain autonomy of administration, first of all under a Ducal Gastaldo, and later under a Podestà.

It had its own Council and the names of the original families of the island were inscribed in a Golden Book, and enjoyed special privileges; among other things, a Venetian nobleman might marry the daughter of a master glass craftsman without endangering or diminishing the degree of his own nobility.

The period in which the working of glass was begun in Venice, in the estuary and most particularly in Murano, is not known.

The art, handed down by the Romans and imported by various travellers, probably received a fresh impulse from the frequent contacts Venice had with the Eastern world consequent on its maritime traffic.

For fear of fires, which were so disastrous in those days when the buildings of the city were mostly of wood, the Republic gave orders that the glass factories operating in Venice should all be transferred to Murano.

The island therefore became the place where all the furnaces were assembled and the working of glass became the symbol and at the same time the most important source of revenue of the island, the population of which increased considerably.

18 Murano
19 Barovier Bowl, Glass Museum
20 Sixteenth century plate, Glass Museum

SANTA MARIA E DONATO: a Byzantine-Veneto basilica

At the end of Fondamenta Giustiniani stands the church of Santa Maria e Donato, of ancient construction, and re-built in the 12th Century; it was consecrated in 1140.
It is built to a basilical plan, with three naves. The ship's keel ceiling is of the beginning of the 15th Century.
The splendid floor in polychrome mosaic and the huge mosaic in the bowl of the apse are contemporary with the building of this church.

The simplicity of the basilical-type façade is in sharp contrast with the external architectonic solution of the apsidal part, fantastically enriched by the motives of the sham colonnade with deep niches of the first order and of the upper gallery. The isolated bell-tower stands apart in the square, an extremely poignant element in the complex of the environment.

21

22

**The Grand Canal in miniature.
Factories, palaces, vegetable and flower gardens, churches, monasteries. Traces and memories of an antique splendour**

21 Murano, apse of Santa Maria e Donato
22 Murano, eighteenth century houses

9

BETWEEN SEA AND LAGOON

A STRIP OF LAND PLACED IN
DEFENCE OF VENICE AND
ITS NATURAL EQUILIBRIUM

A DEFENCE AGAINST THE
SEA:

THE MURAZZI

The Republic began the building of
the sea-walls (Murazzi) in 1744; it
is a huge sea defensive work with
enormous blocks of stone, conceived
in 1716 by the cosmographer
Vincenzo Coronelli and carried out
under the direction of the Venetian
mathematician Bernardino Zendrini.
The works came to an end in 1782
shortly before the fall of the
Republic, which, although hard up,
found the necessary funds for this
colossal work of engineering
which saved the city from the
inroads of the sea.

24

THE PORT AND THE
CHURCH OF SAN NICOLÓ

'The mouth of the port with entrance
to the lagoon, was in ancient times
furnished with two forts, Castel
Vecchio (which no longer exists
to-day) and Castel Nuovo, which
was built in 1543 to the plans of the
architect Michele Sanmicheli.
St. Nicolò, marks the northern
extremity of the island of Lido, that
is of that long, narrow strip of land
which closes the lagoon as far as
the port of Chioggia.

The Church of St. Nicolò was
founded, together with the monastery,
by the Benedictine monks about
half-way through the 11th Century
(about 1043).
The Church of St. Mark not being
available because it was being built
at the time, here Doge Domenico
Selvo was elected in 1071.
The fabric was re-built in 1626, the
façade remaining uncompleted.
Traces of the primitive church
remain, as well as transformations in
the Gothic period, together with
the Renaissance cloister (1530).

The island of Lido, which prior to
the first world war was almost
devoid of buildings, has within
the last fifty years undergone a rapid
building development, extending as
far as Malamocco.
In the years between the wars, it
quickly became one of the most
renowned seaside resorts in the
world mecca of a tourism for the
« élite » attracted here by glamorous
international exhibitions.

SAN LAZZARO
a sure refuge for the
Armenian community
against the persecutions
in the East.

A community of Armenian brethren
live to-day on the island of
San Lazzaro degli Armeni.
The island, which at first was used
by the Republic as a hospice for sick
pilgrims on their way to the Holy
Land, and later as a lazaretto
dedicated to St. Lazarus, the patron
saint of lepers, was assigned in
1717 to an Armenian nobleman, the
monk Manug di Pietro, known as
Mechitar, a refugee from Methoni
invaded by the Turks. Here he
founded a Benedictine monastery
to house his fellow-countrymen,
refugees like himself from the
persecutions in the East.

25

24 The Lido and the port of S. Nicolò
25 San Lazzaro
26 Chioggia
27, 28 Pellestrina

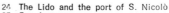

26

In addition to the port of the Alberoni there are the two characteristic and fascinating villages of S. Pietro in Volta and Pellestrina, with their modest, colourful houses aligned along the strip of lagoon and protected in the rear, after a narrow strip of ground devoted to vegetable gardens, by the sea-wall of the « Murazzi ». Hereabouts it appears that there used to be the ports of Albiola and Pastene which were buried as a result of natural causes. The town which rose here took the name of Portosecco. Pellestrina was destroyed in 1380, during the Genoese war, but following the Venetian victory, it was re-built and given the same characteristics it had had before.

CHIOGGIA
AN ANCIENT FISHERMEN'S TOWN

SOTTOMARINA
A MODERN BATHING RESORT

Chioggia is one of the most important fishing centres of the upper Adriatic, situated between the lagoon and the sea. Of very ancient origin, with the name of Fossa Clodia, it was populated by fishermen and salters. It is a little Venice in its urbanistic and building plan; the canals, the largest of which goes right through the centre, are animated by moored « bragozzi » those characteristic fishing vessels with their tall, colourful sails.
The churches are numerous, maintaining in some parts remains of their ancient origin; along the main street is the Granary, a Gothic building of 1322.
Sottomarina, the last beach of the upper arch of the Adriatic, has completely eliminated its one-time appearance substituting it with that of a modern bathing resort.

SAN PIETRO IN VOLTA AND PELLESTRINA lagoon fishermen and market gardeners.

27

28

THE LAYOUT OF VENICE

The development of the city of Venice is closely linked with its political and commercial relations with the East, and most particularly with Constantinople.

Once having gone through the first period of establishing itself, and reached a certain autonomy and security, Venice replaced its poor houses of brick, wood and dried mud, and its buildings of a defensive nature, and its turretted castles, with a new, richer kind of building, the models of which were obviously of Byzantine derivation.

In their voyages to the cities of the Eastern Mediterranean, or to those of the Veneto or Dalmatian hinterland, the Venetians, in addition to carrying on their business, surveyed the culture of these civilizations.

Then returning to Venice they brought not only descriptions of the churches and mansions, but also the material itself, to be used again on the façades of their buildings. Columns, capitals, precious marbles all found a place in the holds of their ships, together with stuffs and spices.

Artisans from the East and from Ravenna were summoned to the city, either by the State, or by private individuals, to superintend the works, and it was they who initiated the new local experts into architectonic and decorative secrets and practice.

29

30

CAMPO, CALLE, FONDAMENTA, CAMPIELLO

CANAL AND RIO

31

32

29 Rio at Burano
30 Rio del Lovo
31 Rio di S. Barnaba
32 Rio Pesaro

Thus the appearance of the city in the earliest centuries was characterized by the Byzantine style. Not much remains in the city of this building activity.

This is the epoch of the great Doges, of the Orseolo, of Domenico Contarini and Sebastiano Ziani. Alongside the building work, proceeded at equal pace the systemization of the swampy territories, ponds were drained, roads were marked out and the various islets were united by more and more wooden bridges, until an urban network came into being. We are now just about half-way through the 13th Century. Starting from this time, the city was taking on an architectonic shape that followed the taste and culture of the rest of Italy, interpreted in a particular manner, which was determined by past tradition and by the particular environment in which such artistic activity was expressing itself.

33

SALIZZADA, CORTE, PISCINA, PONTE, RIO TERRÀ, RAMO, RUGA

34

37

33 Rio di S. Tomà
34 Rio del Gaffaro
35 Rio dei Mendicanti
36 Campo and Scuola of San Tomà
37 Rio delle Beccherie

PIAZZA SAN MARCO
POLITICAL RELIGIOUS AND SOCIAL CENTRE OF THE SERENISSIMA

The present form of St. Mark's Square, political, religious and social nucleus of the city, developed during the course of the ten centuries of the history of the Venetian Republic. Notwithstanding the numerous and inevitable transformations of the buildings composing it, the square, in its totality still maintains a unitary character, even while articulated in two large inter-communicating spaces, the Piazza itself, and the Piazzetta, adjoining to the wide basin of the lagoon, defined in perspective by the contours of the islands of St. George and of the Giudecca.
On to these spaces gaze the various buildings, each one discharging its function of representing and housing the principal political and social structures of the city. The first layout of the city goes back to the origins of the dogedom, that is to the beginning of the 9th Century.

With the growth in power of Venice, the square took on an ever greater richness of appearance.
The Doge Sebastiano Ziani (1172-1178) provided for a new re-building, filling in the Batario canal, and thus doubling the space in front of the Basilica.
The two columns which terminate the space of the little square towards the basin belong to this epoch. They consist of two monoliths brought from the East, which were raised in the 12th Century on stepped octagonal bases.
The buildings in the Square were losing their defensive appearance, this applies particularly to the Ducal Palace, to open externally in new galleried forms.

At the end of the 13th Century the necessity of a radical reconstruction of the Palace was envisaged.
The works were begun towards the half of the 14th Century when the entire wing of the Palace towards the basin was renewed, taking in the former fabric. The continuous arcade was developed on which rests the great volume of the Hall of the Great Council.
Under the dogeship of Francesco Foscari, from 1424, began the building of that part of the edifice which runs from the sixth arcade to the Porta della Carta.

THE WINGED LION OF ST. MARK
EMBLEMATIC FIGURE OF THE POWER OF THE STATE IN FAITH.

38

39

THE PALACE OF THE DOGES
THE BASILICA OF ST. MARK
THE PROCURATIE
THE LIBRARY
THE MINT
THE PRISONS
THE GRANARIES
THE CLOCK TOWER
THE LOGGETTA

The basilica of St. Mark, too, erected in the place of the older church of St. Theodore, had a good three rebuildings in early centuries. The first was erected after 811 by the Doge Angelo Partecipazio; the second after 976, during the dogeship of Pietro IV Candiano and finally the last with Domenico Contarini in 1063, which is the one still in existence, although the continuous work of embellishment and decoration in succeeding centuries have completely changed its former aspect.
Along the sides of the Square other buildings went up, among them the seat of the Canons of St. Mark, the houses of the Procurators of St. Mark, the church of St. Geminiano and the Orseolo Hospice.
Facing the Piazzetta, a series of buildings containing the bakehouse, the bakery, the butcher and the Mint. One of the characteristics of those early centuries of the dukedom was the presence in both the Piazza and the Piazzetta of numerous shops backing on to the fronts of buildings or hollowed out under the arcades.

Towards the end of the 15th Century began that wonderful transformation of the buildings of the city and in particular of St. Mark's Square.
A part of the Byzantine houses of the Procurators of St. Mark's were demolished between 1496 and 1499 to build the Clock Tower.
Between 1469 and 1530, Mauro Codussi, Bartolomeo Bon and Guglielmo de' Grigi re-built the Procuratie Vecchie; then in the course of the 16th Century came the building of the Mint, the Library and finally, in the 17th Century, came the building of the Procuratie Nuove.
It was Sansovino who formulated the new planimetric design of the Piazza which to a great extent follows the pre-existing design with the exception of the part around the bell-tower which is completely free at its base except for the elegant little Loggia also designed by Sansovino. It was then Scamozzi who continued and Longhena who concluded the building programme of the renewal which was begun in the time of the Renaissance.

On the side opposite the church of St. Mark, the same Sansovino had renewed the ancient church of St. Geminiano.

It was destroyed in the early years of the 19th Century when it was the wish to have a large hall in the Piazza (nowadays called « Napoleonic ») for receptions.
The old paving of the Square of St. Mark, in red brick laid herring-bone style remained unaltered from 1264 to the beginning of the 18th Century, when, following the taste of the times, it was wished to give the Square a more elegant appearance, substituting the bricks with the grey trachyte from the Euganean Hills. Andrea Tirali superintended this work, from 1722 to 1735.

38 Lion in a « moleca » (crab)
39 Piazza San Marco and the Punta della Dogana
40 Piazza San Marco

41

THE PALACE OF THE DOGE

THE SPLENDID SEAT OF GOVERNMENT

When in 810 Angelo Partecipazio transferred the government from Malamocco to the islands of Rivoaltus, it was necessary to pick out a precise area on which to build the seat of the organs of this new state.

The first choice of a spot in front of which opened a wide basin where the most important waterways of communication flowed together and had their centre, proved substantially exact, since it was never from that time under discussion. The Ducal Palace, therefore, rose at the same time as Venice itself, that is to say, in the second decade of the 9th Century. The Most Serene Republic always placed particular attention on the building evolution of the Palace and in the various centuries spent enormous sums of money so that its appearance, external and internal might be a concrete expression of an ideal conception, as is that of the political state.

42

43

16

THE GREAT COUNCIL
THE SENATE
THE COUNCIL OF TEN
QUARANTIA CIVIL
QUARANTIA CRIMINAL

The reconstruction we can make to-day of this earliest fabric is based on only a few elements; it had to be a building of a purely defensive character, very much resembling a medieval castle, on a more or less square plan. More precisely, a circle of high walls with strong keeps at the corners facing the basin and with a fortified entrance.

Little by little as the Republic continued to make itself more secure, and powerful, the architecture of the Palace was losing its defensive appearance to assume the more open forms of Veneto-Byzantine architecture.

The dogeship of Sebastiano Ziani is characterized by an exceptional building activity in the city.

The Palace took on a new aspect and new dimensions between 1272 and 1278 with the building of the new « City Hall », of the Palace « ad ius reddendum » towards the Piazzetta and the arrangement of rooms fit for other magistracies.

But with the growth of importance of the greatest Venetian institution and the ever-growing exigencies of a suitable seat which would reflect the ease and power attained by the ruling class, towards the year 1340, bringing all uncertainties to an end, it was decided to build a new and splendid Hall of the Great Council.

In the year 1365 the works must have been to a great extent at an end, since it was then that the Paduan artist Guariento was commissioned to fresco the end wall with the « The Coronation of the Virgin ».

41 The Piazzetta
42 Doge Pietro Loredan, J. Tintoretto (Doge's Palace)
43 St. Mark's Basin
44 « Noah and his sons » (Doge's Palace)
45 Doge's Palace

45

The architectonic structure of the huge central window was brought to an end only in the year 1404, the work of Pier Paolo delle Masegne. The names of the principal artists in this architectonic undertaking at the Ducal Palace as they appear in documents are few: Filippo Calendario and Pietro Basegio.

In 1424, under the dogeship of Francesco Foscari, it was decided to renew the Palace of Justice towards the Piazzetta, following the forms and solutions adopted in the previous century, so that the entire seat of Government appeared in all its impressive unity.

Let us pause for a moment before the beautiful plastic solutions which decorate the Palace, starting at the corner towards the Canal. « The Drunkenness of Noah » with his sons Shem, Ham and Japheth; above at the height of the loggia is « The Archangel Raphael with Tobias », symbol of commerce.

On the corner towards the Piazzetta « The progenitors, Adam and Eve » under the tree with the serpent and on high « The Archangel Michael » with the unsheathed sword, the symbol of war.

The sculpture of the third corner near the Porta della Carta (Door of the paper), « The Judgement of King Solomon », is a stupendous marble group alluding to Justice, which latest attributions ascribe to the chisel of Jacopo della Quercia, though previously thought to be by Pietro Lamberti.

Above, the « Archangel Gabriel » symbolises Peace.

48

46 Doge's Palace, corner between the Basin and the Piazzetta
47 Capital in the arcading
48 Capital (detail)
49 The four-lobed traceries of the Foscari Loggia
50 Doge Francesco Foscari, L. Bastiani (Correr Museum)

18

49

Many of the capitals of the arcade, both the most ancient towards the basin and those more recent towards the Piazzetta, have been substituted by copies during a grandiose restoration carried out at the beginning of the 20th Century. Here we give a rapid description of the subjects dealt with, starting from the corner towards the Canal:

Vices
Birds
Vices and Virtues
Heads of Lions
Animals
Love tournament

Heads of Men
Sages
The planets and the creation of man
The Saint martyrs-sculptors
Animals with prey
Trades
The ages of man
The peoples
A love story
Infancy and the Barber's art
Birds
Heads of Knights and Crusaders
Infancy
Heads of Emperors
Heads of women
Vices and Virtues
Musicians and monsters
Virtues

Here ends the oldest series which goes back to the building of that part of the Palace which contains the Hall of the Great Council. On the part built later, under the dogeship of the Foscari:
The months of the year
Love tournament
Baskets of fruit
Vices and Virtues
Virtues
Vices
Musicians and monsters
Education
Vices and Virtues
Birds
Children
The Law-givers

50

THE DOGE
A representative and symbolic figure

Even in the complexity of the various arrangements we can assign specific functions to the various parts of the Palace: the part towards the Canal housed the apartment of the Doge; the successive group of halls housed the various magistracies of Venice, such as the College and the Senate; then came the Palace of Justice with the Court rooms and the Dungeons (the Wells and the Leads), in the corner towards the Ponte della Paglia, the Armoury. The wing towards the lagoon houses the huge Hall of the Great Council. In the wing towards the Piazzetta, the Voting Hall, which before the building of the Marciana Library was also used as a Library.

19

THE PORTA DELLA CARTA

THE FOSCARI ARCH

THE GIANTS' STAIRCASE

A LOGGIA IN THE COURTYARD

THE GOLDEN STAIRCASE

The principal entrance to the Palace is through the Porta della Carta, built between 1438 and 1443 by Giovanni and Bartolomeo Bon in flamboyant Gothic style.

At one time it was painted in blue, gold and red.

On his knees before the winged lion, the figure of the Doge Francesco Foscari. The one we see to-day is a copy of the original statue, destroyed at the time of the fall of the Republic.

The only fragment remaining is the very beautiful head of Foscari, preserved in the Museo dell'Opera together with the original capitals.

The Porta della Carta leads directly to the Foscari Entrance Hall.

Facing it is the Renaissance Stairway of the Giants, planned and built by Antonio Rizzo, at the beginning of 1483.

On the upper landing of the Stairway the first official investiture of the Doge took place before he was presented to the people.

The two statues on the balustrade, Mars and Neptune, are a late work by Jacopo Sansovino.

51

52

On the right opens the great courtyard.

The two brick façades to be seen corresponding to the Hall of the Great Council and the Voting Hall, go back to the 14th and 15th Centuries.

The third façade is Renaissance; it was built after the great fire of 1483. This last was planned and begun by Antonio Rizzo, and then from 1498 by the Lombardos; after the year 1516 the work was completed by Antonio Abbondi, known as the Scarpagnino.

Contemporaneously was built the new façade on Rio di Palazzo.

Some parts of the courtyard were terminated at the beginning of the 17th Century by the intervention of Monopola who opened up the ground floor arcading on the two old fronts. From one of the inside loggias one reaches the Halls through the highly decorated « Golden Stairway ».

The building was begun under the dogeship of Andrea Gritti (1523-1539) to the plan of Jacopo Sansovino and finished by Scarpagnino in 1559.

Numerous artists collaborated in the carrying out of the work: the marble statues are by Tiziano Aspetti; the stuccoes of the vault by Alessandro Vittoria; the frescoes of the panels by Battista Franco.

51 « Doge F. Foscari », fragment (Museum of works)
52 The Paper Gate
53 The Giants' Staircase, A. Rizzo
54 The Giants' Staircase (detail)
55 « Eve », A. Rizzo
56 The Golden Staircase. J. Sansovino

53

54

55

56

57

THE DOGE'S APARTMENT

58

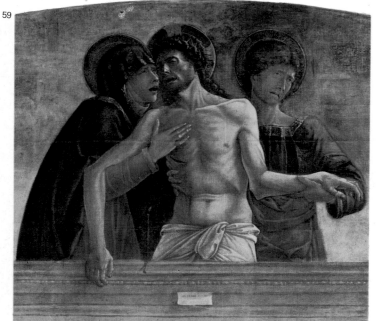

59

The Hall of the Scarlatti was used as an antechamber of the Ducal Counsellors.
In the Hall of the Shield or of the Maps, with numerous geographical maps on the walls, the work of Francesco Grisellini and Giustino Menescardi, the Doge used to entertain guests.
From the Hall of Philosophers, a small stair allowed the Doge to go up directly into the Senate Hall.
On the wall above the door is a fresco by Titian, representing « St. Christopher » executed in the years 1523-1524.
In the Grimani and Erizzo Halls are preserved the wooden ceilings of the end of the 15th Century, the work of the wood-carving Fratelli of Faenza.
The numerous fireplaces in all the rooms of the apartment are the work of the Lombardos; the decorated stucco canopies are later additions.
In the next three rooms used now as a Picture Gallery, there is a series of paintings from various schools, among them the « Christ Mourned » by Giovanni Bellini, the « Christ Derided » by Q. Matsys, the « Inferno » by Civetta; the triptychs of « St. Jerome » and of « St. Juliana », the « Paradise » and the « Inferno » are all painted by Hieronymus Bosch.
The « Winged Lion » is by Vittore Carpaccio.

THE ROOM OF THE
SCARLATTI

THE ROOM OF THE SHIELD

THE GRIMANI ROOM

THE ERIZZO ROOM

THE PRIULI ROOM

THE PHILOSOPHERS' HALL

THE HALL OF THE SQUIRES

57 « Winged Lion », V. Carpaccio
58 The Erizzo Room
59 « Christ Mourned », G. Bellini (detail)
60 « Triptych of Santa Liberata », J. Bosch
61 « Christ Derided », Q. Matsys (detail)
 J. Tintoretto (detail)
62 « St. Christopher », Titian (detail)

60

61

62

THE HALL OF THE FOUR DOORS

64

The Hall of the Four Doors was restored and decorated to the design of Andrea Palladio after the fire of 1574.

In the panels of the ceiling, richly decorated with stuccoes, the work of Giovanni Cambi and of Master Baldissera, there are frescoes by Tintoretto representing symbolically the power of Venice.

On the walls are paintings by Titian « The Doge Grimani worships the Faith », by Caliari « The Doge Pasquale Cicogna receives gifts from the Persian Ambassadors », by Vicentino « The arrival in Venice of Henry III of France ».

The place mirrors very clearly its function as Waiting Room and passage as regards the adjacent rooms.

This special function is emphasized by the four doors which open symmetrically along the two longer walls.

The portals, to the design of Palladio, consist of two detached columns which support the pediment, crowned by three statues representing respectively:

Door to the Square Vestibule: *Secrecy, Faithfulness, Diligence* (Giulio del Moro)

Door to the Council of Ten: *Religion, Justice, Authority* (Francesco Castelli)

Door to the Senate Hall: *War, Pallas, Peace* (Gerolamo Campagna)

Door to the College: *Eloquence, Vigilance, Fluency* (Alessandro Vittoria)

63 Hall of the Four Doors
64 « Arrival of Henry III », A. Vicentino (detail)
65 « The Rape of Europa » P. Veronese
66 Room of the Antecollege
67 « The finding of Ariadne », J. Tintoretto
68 « Pallas and Mars », J. Tintoretto
69 « The Forge of Vulcan », J. Tintoretto
70 « Mercury and the Graces », J. Tintoretto

THE HALL OF THE ANTECOLLEGE

This hall was used as an ante-room for embassies and delegations waiting to be received by the Signoria.
The Hall of the Ante-College, is reminiscent of the Hall of Four Doors in the taste of its stucco decoration.
Tiziano Aspetti was the sculptor of the telamones and the frieze of the mantelpiece. On the walls are four paintings executed by Tintoretto around 1577. « The Forge of Vulcan », « Mercury and the Graces », « Pallas repulses Mars », « The Re-discovery of Ariadne »; other canvases by Veronese, such as « The Rape of Europa », and finally « The return of Jacob from Canaan » by Jacopo Bassano.

65

67

68

66

69

70

25

THE HALL OF THE COLLEGE

This Magistracy had the task of handling the preliminary discussions of matters to be presented to the Senate. It also had the difficult task of dealing with the Roman Church; part of the judicial power was delegated to it.

In fact, it had to settle controversies in connection with ecclesiastical benefices, privileges of dependent towns, tolls, contracts, etc.

In 1526 its powers were considerably increased, since with apparently only formal functions such as presenting official orders and decrees, it could also withhold from the Senate certain proceedings which it considered must be kept secret. Another function, important because of the matters dealt with at times, but in general of a formal, public character, was to receive and to grant hearings to the foreign delegations who from time to time arrived in Venice.

71

THE DECORATIVE SCHEME WAS COMPLETELY RENEWED OWING TO A FIRE

72

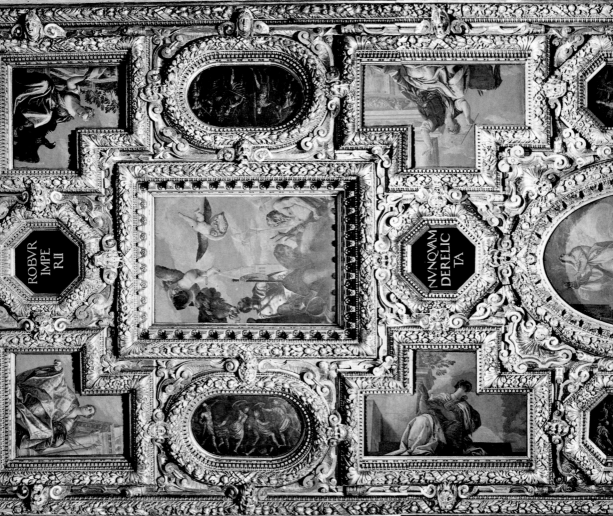

The Hall of the College where there
is a noticeable unity about the
decorative scheme, was planned, as
was the Hall of the Senate, by Andrea
Palladio and Giovan Antonio
Rusconi under the direction of
Antonio Da Ponte, following the
fire that occurred in 1574.
The ceiling, a work carried out
by Francesco Bello and Andrea
Faentin between 1577 and 1578,
forms a frame for numerous panels
with paintings by Paolo Veronese.
In the central panels are « Mars
and Neptune », « Faith », « Justice
and Peace render homage to
Venice », and then in the side
panels, symbolic figures such as
« Fidelity », « Prosperity »,
« Meekness », « Simplicity » and
most famous of all, « Dialectics ».
On the walls above the original
seats: « Sebastiano Venier after
the Battle of Lepanto » by Paolo
Veronese, painted in 1578; the other
paintings are by Tintoretto and
represent the Doges Alvise Mocenigo,
Nicolò Da Ponte, Francesco Donà
and Andrea Gritti in various
attitudes of thanks to the Virgin
and Saints.

73

71 « The Marriage of St. Catherine »,
   J. Tintoretto (detail)
72 Ceiling of the Hall of the College
73 « Sebastiano Venier after Lepanto ».
   P. Veronese (detail)

THE HALL OF THE SENATE OR OF THE " PREGADI "

In the Hall of the Senate met one of the most important magistracies of the Republic, made up of Senators or « Requesteds » because they were requested by the Doge to enter from the nearby Hall of the Four Doors.
The Magistracy of the Senate was instituted in 1229; towards the end of the 14th Century the number of sixty members to be elected annually was established. To the sixty were added the « Zonte » of varying numbers. The attributions of the Senate were many and various and increased as time passed. The assembly discussed all the political doings of the Republic, in particular it had the responsibility of deciding and declaring wars, the nomination of ordinary and extraordinary magistrates, as well as the Patriarch and the Bishops. It also nominated the study commissions for the elaboration of plans and projects of new laws and reforms in administrative, economic, judicial, sanitary matters, ecology of the waters, etc.

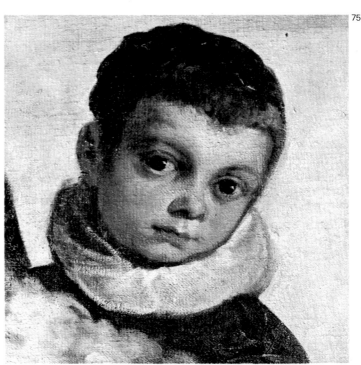

Going again across the Hall of the Four Doors one arrives in the rooms of the Palace of Justice, where the courts used to meet.

The Magistracy of the Council of Ten was instituted in 1319, following the plot hatched up by Bajamonte Tiepolo.

It looked after the security of the State with full jurisdiction over political crimes and to this end had at its disposal a terribly efficient secret police.

The Court consisted of ten members to which were added the Doge and his six Counsellors.

The ceiling of the Hall was executed between 1553 and 1554; the paintings in the panels are all allegorical representations by Giambattista Ponchino, Paolo Veronese and Giambattista Zelotti.

76

The ceiling, planned and executed by Cristoforo Sorte (c. 1581), presents large panels with gilded frames and extremely rich volutes. All the paintings of the Hall were executed between 1585 and 1595, during the dogeship of Pasquale Cicogna.

In the central panel « The Triumph of Venice » is by Jacopo Tintoretto. On the walls, too, are two great clocks with the signs of the zodiac. By Tintoretto, « The dead Christ between the Doges Pietro Lando and Marcantonio Trevisan »; by J. Palma the Y.: « Venice and Doge Venier receive gifts from subject cities », « Doge Pasquale Cicogna praying to the Saviour in the presence of St. Mark », « Allegory of the League of Cambrai » (the Doge Leonardo Loredan and Venice confront the states who participate in the League against Venice).

74 Hall of the Senate
75 « Doge Venier and the subject towns », J. Palma the younger (detail)
76 « The Triumph of Venice ». J. Tintoretto

THE HALL OF THE GREAT COUNCIL

78

The Hall of the Great Council is the largest hall in the entire Ducal Palace; it is 54 metres long, 25 metres wide and 12 metres high. Here used to meet the Great Council, the highest magistracy of the State, whose membership grew from 300 to 1,600.

The first decoration of this Hall with valuable frescoes on the walls (Gentile da Fabriano, Pisanello, Vivarini, Bellini, Carpaccio, Titian, Pordenone, Veronese and Tintoretto) was completely destroyed in the fire which broke out during the night in 1577; later came a radical restoration in the hands of Antonio Da Ponte. The decorative renovations, too, went ahead very rapidly, between 1578 and 1595. Among all the painters who had worked on the decoration of the hall that was destroyed, only Veronese and Tintoretto had the task of participating in the new scheme of decoration.

The series of new paintings, no longer frescoes, but on canvas, imitate for the most part the themes of the earlier paintings.

In the panels of the ceiling the paintings represent the glorification of the Republic and episodes of war and conquest; « The triumph of Venice among the Gods of Mount Olympus » by Paolo Veronese, « The Doge Da Ponte receives an olive-branch from Venice » by Jacopo Tintoretto, « Venice, crowned by Victory, greets her subject provinces » by J. Palma the Younger.

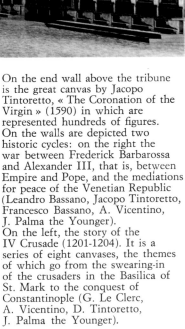

79

THE HALL OF THE SCRUTINIO
HERE THE DOGE WAS ELECTED

80

On the end wall above the tribune
is the great canvas by Jacopo
Tintoretto, « The Coronation of the
Virgin » (1590) in which are
represented hundreds of figures.
On the walls are depicted two
historic cycles: on the right the
war between Frederick Barbarossa
and Alexander III, that is, between
Empire and Pope, and the mediations
for peace of the Venetian Republic
(Leandro Bassano, Jacopo Tintoretto,
Francesco Bassano, A. Vicentino,
J. Palma the Younger).
On the left, the story of the
IV Crusade (1201-1204). It is a
series of eight canvases, the themes
of which go from the swearing-in
of the crusaders in the Basilica of
St. Mark to the conquest of
Constantinople (G. Le Clerc,
A. Vicentino, D. Tintoretto,
J. Palma the Younger).

**THE ASSEMBLY OF THE
VENETIAN ARISTOCRACY
WIELDED LEGISLATIVE POWER
AND ELECTED BY SECRET
BALLOT
THE MEMBERS OF ALL THE
BODIES OF THE GOVERNMENT**

77 Hall of the Great Council
78 « The Battle of Chioggia ».
    P. Veronese (detail)
79 « Doge Sebastiano Ziani about to
    embark against Barbarossa »,
    F. Bassano
80 « The Last Judgement »,
    J. Palma the younger (detail)

The Scrutiny (Voting) Hall, too,
gravely damaged in the same fire
of 1577, was restored and completed
in the ten following years under
the dogeship of Nicolò Da Ponte.
Above the tribune the great painting
depicting « The Last Judgement » was
executed by J. Palma the Younger
between 1587 and 1594.
On the right-hand wall in the
centre is the famous « Battle of
Lepanto » by Andrea Vicentino.

On the end wall, connected with
the 16th Century Foscara Staircase,
was constructed the triumphal arch
dedicated to Francesco Morosini,
known as the Peloponnesiac, to
celebrate his victories in Morea and
in the Peloponnese against the Turks.
The design of the monument is by
Antonio Gaspari.
The paintings of the smaller panels
of the ceiling deal with allegorical
and historical subjects (Aliense,
Bellini, M. Vecellio and G. Licinio)

31

THE ARMOURY

Certainly from the 13th Century and in all probability even in an earlier period, there existed an Armoury in the Palace. The custody of this deposit of arms, known as « munition » was in the hands of the Council of Ten. The importance that the Council attributed to the Armoury causes us to suppose that the material of war was the object of a very costly commerce.
A document of 1317 localizes the place where the Armoury used to be housed, near the old Hall of the Great Council. After that year the seat varied fairly often for the need to have new space and to have better defended and safer places. Towards 1532 came the final transfer into the rooms which even to-day we find given over to the same purpose. In 1609 another place was used for this, on the floor below in the immediate neighbourhood of the Hall of the Great Council known as

81

82

the Armaments Hall (now the Hall of Guariento).
In this, during the sittings, the arms were always kept loaded, ready to be used promptly in case of a revolt or attempts to take over the power.
It was never necessary to use them. Nobody had access to the Armoury save the Overseer of Munitions who obtained the keys daily from the secretary of the Ten.
Sometimes the Halls of the Arms were visited by illustrious personages, but only after special deliberation and always accompanied by some members of the Council

83

84

81 Beaked Sallet
82 Culverin and fuse-urn
83 Pistols with three barrels on revolving cylinders
84 Torture Instruments
85 Morosini Hall
86 Gattamelata's Armour

THE ROOM OF
GATTAMELATA
THE ROOM OF HENRY IV
THE ROOM OF MOROSINI
THE ROOM OF THE
ARQUEBUSES

" WHITE ARMS " AND FIRE-ARMS FOR ATTACK AND DEFENCE, CLOSE COMBAT, TOURNAMENT, AND PARADE.

The arms with which the Council was endowed from the 10th to the 15th Century were preserved and always kept in good order in case of extreme necessity. The majority of these were arms in common use; to these were added others which had a purely decorative interest and were used for parades and particular ceremonies.

Among the armour, let us mention that belonging to the Condottiere Erasmo da Narni, known as the Gattamelata; the equestrian armour of Henry IV of France given by him to the Republic in 1603.

Among the finest pieces in the collection: a beaked sallet, a 15th Century work of Italian armourers; a bronze culverin with floral motifs in relief, an Italian work of the first half of the 16th Century, attributable to Alberghetti; a twenty barrel arquebus signed by G.M. Bergamin; ·a small cannon or mortar with cylindrical breech and five revolver-type barrels; various instruments of torture, and a chastity belt listed in the 1548 inventory as: « iron pants of the wife of the Lord of Padua ».

HALBERDS, MACES, SWORDS, QUIVERS, CULVERINS, FUSE-HOLDERS, DAGGERS, ARQUEBUSES, SPIKED MACES, TWO-HANDED SWORDS, BREAST-PLATES, BOWS, CROSSBOWS, MORIONS, SPEARS, HEAD-PIECES, HORSE-CHAMFRON, BRIGANDINES, PARTISANS, HATCHETS, HELMETS, SLAV SWORDS, SALLETS, MUSKETS, SPIKED SHIELDS, PAVISES, SPIKES, BANNERS, PISTOLS, SHIELDS, LIGHT PISTOLS, SCIMITARS, PIKES, RAPIERS, HAMMERS, STANDARDS, MIXED HALBERDS, RANSEURS, SICKLES, LONG RAPIERS, COMMANDERS' RAPIERS, CANNON, FALCHIONS, BUCKLERS, TARGES, HORSE ARMOUR, FLASKS, BATTLE-AXES, PISTOLS, BEAKED SALLETS.

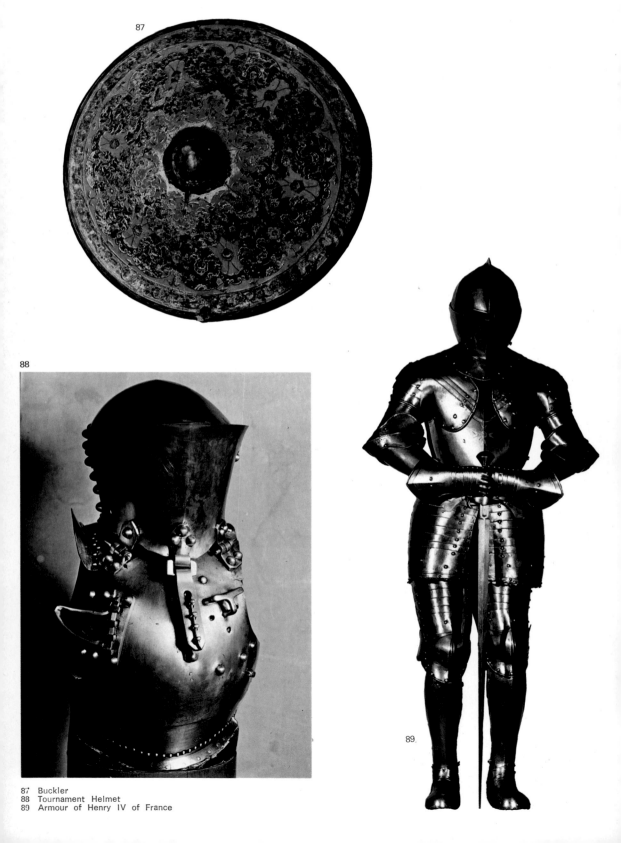

87 Buckler
88 Tournament Helmet
89 Armour of Henry IV of France

THE BRIDGE OF SIGHS

A ROMANTIC NAME FOR A FUNCTIONAL STRUCTURE LINKING TWO BUILDINGS

90

The Bridge of Sighs joins the Ducal Palace to the New Prisons beyond the Rio.
The bridge was built at the beginning of the 17th Century to the design of Antonio Contin.
The denomination « of sighs » is the fruit of the literature of the Romantic Age when the function of the bridge had already ended.
The New Prisons beyond the Rio were built in three periods successively from 1566 to the early years of the 17th Century.
The part of the building facing Riva degli Schiavoni was carried out following the project of Antonio Da Ponte.
Returning to the Ducal Palace across the second passage of the Bridge of Sighs one enters the Avogaria, a series of rooms, once seats of numerous magistracies.
At the end of our way we find the Pozzi (Wells), the only prisons remaining inside the Palace, particularly unhealthy because of the extreme humidity due to their location on the ground floor.
One of these cells still preserves the wooden panelling as it used to be, and the plank which served prisoners as a bed.

91

THE LION'S MOUTH

In various parts of the Palace along the walls of the loggia, in the Halls of the Bussola and of the Quarantia Criminal, various lions' mouths are built into the walls, special receptacles for secret denunciations.
The denomination comes from the fact that on the exterior there was the sculpture of a lion's head, whose open mouth constituted the mouth of the receptacle itself.
Every Magistracy, whether it watched over the quiet and safety of the State, or whether it punished common crimes, or whether it administered the finances, had its own lion's mouth.

92

DENONTIE SECRETE

90 The Bridge of Sighs
91 The Palace of the Prisons
92 Lion's Mouth

35

THE BASILICA OF ST. MARK

THE DUCAL CHAPEL

In 832 came the consecration of the first Church dedicated to the Evangelist St. Mark, whose remains, according to legend had been purloined by two Venetian navigators from a monastery in Alexandria in Egypt and brought to Venice. The evangelical symbol of the winged lion became the symbol of the city while St. Mark became its Patron Saint. The church, known as that of the Partecipàzio because it was wished for and built by Angelo Partecipazio whose family between 811 and 939 gave all of seven doges to the city, was destroyed in the fire of 976, when the people in revolt, to drive out Doge Pietro IV Candiano, set fire to the Ducal Castle.

His successor, Pietro Orseolo began the rebuilding and restoration of the edifices destroyed. In 1063, under the dogeship of Domenico Contarini, the works for the third and last re-building of the Basilica of St. Mark were begun. In 1071, on the death of the Doge, the rebuilding was completed in its essential structural parts and in 1094 it was consecrated. This is the church still in existence to-day, enriched, however, later by an unceasing work of decoration and marble panelling, and also of mosaics. Then it appeared, although grandiose, bare and severe with its unadorned brick structure.

A CONTINUOUS SYSTEMATIC INTELLIGENT WORK SHIFTING AND RE-USING MATERIALS

MARBLES, COLUMNS, CAPITALS, PIERCED MARBLE PANELS, LOW-RELIEFS, STATUES, CORNICES, SHEATHING THE ANCIENT AND STOUT STRUCTURE.

95

FOUR GOLDEN HORSES

96

The works of completion did not end until the 15th Century with the splendid crowning of foliage, the pinnacles and the little niches on the upper arches of the façade. In earlier centuries was arranged the double order of columns and capitals between the five great portals, after which were executed the low reliefs of the arches of the main portal; and the low semi-spherical domes were covered with a second cupola in lead independent of the inner one and crowned by a lantern in oriental taste.

97

93 The Lantern of the Dome
94 The Façade of the Basilica of S. Mark
95 The « horses » on the façade
96 The Central Doorway
97 Bas-relief on the side façade

37

98

99

THREE SUCCESSIVE RECONSTRUCTIONS AND A WORK OF COMPLETION AND OF DECORATIVE ENRICHMENT LASTING CENTURIES

The plan is of a Greek cross. The atrium or narthex goes around the three sides of the lower extremity of the cross. The pilasters of the nave support the five large domes. Externally the Church is seen to be in two orders. Between the two orders runs the balcony in the centre of which are the four bronze horses brought from Byzantium after the conquest of the city during the IV Crusade. In the lower order on the left is the arch of St. Alipius added to the building in the 13th Century. In the bowl of the first portal is preserved the only mosaic remaining of the original cycle of mosaics of the façade, representing the « Transport of the body of St. Mark into the Basilica » (the only reminder of what the old church was like). In the interior and exterior fillets of the arches of the central portal a very important series of sculptures of the early 12th Century. In order from the smallest arch to the largest: animals confronted or fighting within floral motives; scenes of hunting or of war; the months of the year and the signs of the zodiac; symbolical representations of the virtues and beatitudes; the Venetian crafts; and then between volutes and pierced paterae, the prophets and Christ blessing. In the corner near the Porta della Carta, the group of the Tetrarchs, known as « Moors »; four figures of warriors in porphyry which seem to portray the emperors who were colleagues of Diocletian. On the left, isolated, the two pilasters from Acre, Venetian booty of war after the conquest of St. John of Acre in Syria in 1256.

THE CAMPANILE OF SAN MARCO

The Bell-tower of St. Mark's has been restored many times, and in part transformed, above all in the terminal part; in 1902 it suddenly crashed to earth, but immediately afterwards was re-built and finished in 1912. Among the five bells, that known as the « marangona » is famous, its name deriving from the fact that it rang at the beginning and ending of the working day of the « Marangoni », that is to say, the carpenters and in general of the skilled workers of all the arts and corporations.

100

102

101

103

98 « Procession in the Piazza San Marco », Gentile Bellini (detail)
99 One of the side doors on the façade
100 The Façade on the Piazzetta del Leoncini
101 The transept Rose window
102 The Campanile of San Marco
103 The façade on the Piazzetta

104

105

THE TETRARCHS

The very fine group of Tetrarchs known commonly as « I mori » — the moors — represents four warriors armed with swords, in the act of meeting and embracing.
The work is in red porphyry.
The figures, according to current interpretation, represent the four emperors, colleagues during the time of Diocletian and must once have served as a support to the architrave of a doorway.
In the holes, still visible in the headpieces, crowns must have been fixed, symbols of their royal rank.
Popular legend, on the other hand, holds that these figures are four

Saracens — moors — who wanted to steal the treasure in the Basilica of St. Mark.
Isolated in front of the façade on the Piazzetta, there are two beautiful square pillars brought as war trophies from the East by the Venetians.
In fact these very interesting examples of VI century Syrian art, were stolen from the church of Santa Saba and put onto the ships leaving for Venice after the sack of Saint John of Acre and the defeat of the Genoese.

106

Passing inside the Basilica, the front part and the left wing of the narthex are spaced rhythmically with arches alternating with small blind domes, while the right wing is closed and houses the Zen Chapel and the Baptistery. The vaults are completely covered with mosaics, executed from the beginning of the 13th Century. These mosaics illustrate « The creation of the World » (in 24 episodes), « The building of the Tower of Babel », « The Story of Abraham », « The Story of Joseph », « Story of Moses ». Through the middle portal one arrives in the real interior of the Church.

One is amazed above all by the sense of sanctity and ancient religiosity of this place, where the massive structure and the great beauty of the mosaic surfaces blend together and are equilibrated in a rare harmony.

This exceptional mosaic work begun during the Dogeship of Domenico Selvo (1071-1084) of which fragments remain, was continued and developed in the 12th and 13th Centuries; and it covers a great part of the interior surfaces.

Some parts were renewed later because of the deterioration of the oldest ones, but mostly retaining the original subjects.

The mosaics extend over a surface of about 4,500 square metres.

107

A Greek cross plan with an atrium along the sides of the foot of the cross. The five cupolas cover each arm and the central intersection.

108

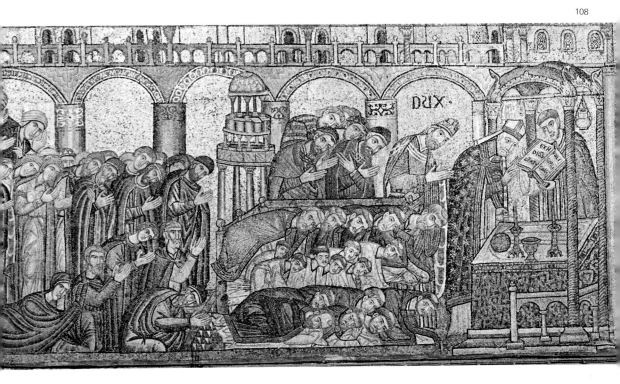

104 The lefthand side door
105 The « Tetrarchs ».
106 Bas-reliefs on the side façade
107 « The Prayer in the Garden », mosaic
108 « The finding of the body of St Mark », mosaic

41

109 « The Crucifixion », mosaic
110 « The kiss of Judas », mosaic
111 « St. Mark », mosaic
112 « Noah's Ark », mosaic
113 Interior
114 The dome of the Chancel

THE MOSAICS OF THE ATRIUM AND THE NAVE

113

A CYCLE OF MOSAICS OF VAST EXTENT AND OF INCOMPARABLE BEAUTY.
THE FASCINATION OF THE COLOUR AND THE GOLD.

Let us mention briefly the themes dealt with and the period of the mosaics of the nave.
Starting at the entrance, the Arch of Paradise: « Scene of the Last Judgement » (16th Century).
Arch of the Apocalypse: « Descent of the Holy Spirit upon the Apostles » (12th Century).
In the two lateral naves are treated the salient facts in the « Life of the Apostles » and their martyrdom. While the mosaics in the left-hand lateral nave were redone in the 16th Century and some in the 17th Century, those in the right-hand lateral nave are still the original ones of the 12th and 13th Century. On the end walls, on the left « Paradise with the Trinity »; on the right, « Christ praying in the Garden » both of the 13th Century. On the great central arch « The Passion of Christ » is shown in five episodes (middle 13th Century). In the great central dome known as that of the Ascension, predominates the figure of Christ in Glory surrounded by Angels, by the Virgin, by the 12 Apostles, by figures symbolizing the Virtues and the Beatitudes, and lastly by the Evangelists and the four sacred rivers. These mosaics are of the first half of the 13th Century.

114

43

THE CHAPEL OF THE MASCOLI

THE CHAPEL OF SANT'ISIDORO

THE CRYPT

The Chapel of St. Isidore, on a rectangular plan with a barrel vault, is also decorated with important mosaics of the 14th Century dealing with « Episodes in the life of St. Isidore » and « The transport of the Saint's body from Chios to Venice » (in 1125, under the Doge Domenico Michiel).
To one side opens the Chapel of the Madonna of the Mascoli, belonging to a Venetian fraternity consisting only of men.
An important cycle is that of the mosaics representing « Episodes in the life of the Virgin » begun by Michele Giambono around 1430 and finished, it seems, on designs by Jacopo Bellini, Andrea Mantegna and Andrea del Castagno.

THE BAPTISTERY

The Baptistery, also called the Church of the Putti, underwent transformations in the 14th Century. The baptismal font was constructed to a plan by Jacopo Sansovino towards the middle of the 16th Century.
The numerous mosaics on the walls and in the dome go back to the middle of the 14th Century and deal with « The Life of St. John the Baptist » and « The infancy of Christ ».

118

119

120

THE ROOD SCREEN IN FRONT OF THE CHANCEL

THE TREASURY OF THE BASILICA

122

After the Baptistery, let us visit
the Treasury of St. Mark, collected
in three adjoining rooms, the
Sanctuary, the Ante-Treasury and the
Treasury. In these rooms is to be
seen one of the richest and most
important collections of Byzantine
and oriental goldsmithery, going
back mostly to the period following
the conquest of Constantinople and
that of Tyre on the part of the
Venetians.

120 Dome of the Baptistery
121 « The three Marys »,
     mosaic (det.)
122 The Golden Altarpiece
123, 124 The Golden
     Altarpiece (detail)

121

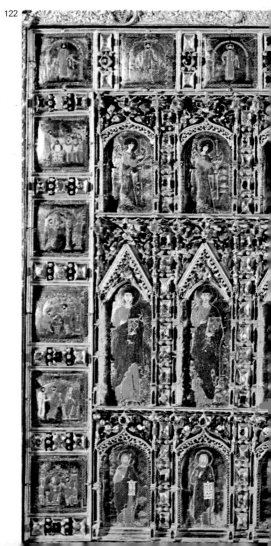

THE GOLDEN ALTAR SCREEN

An exceptional work of goldsmithery.

The Presbytery is divided from the nave by the Gothic Rood screen, which carries above the architrave statues of the Virgin, of St. John the Evangelist and of the Twelve Apostles, the work of the Delle Masegnes (1394).
On the main altar is the Gold Altarpiece, rectangular in form (3.50 x 1.40), goldsmiths' work of inestimable value, where the figures of Saints and Virgins liven up the decorative scheme, enriched then by enamels, and set with jewels.
The work is the fruit of a labour long protracted in time; it assumed its present aspect in the 14th Century.

125

THE PROCURATIE VECCHIE AND THE PROCURATIE NUOVE

The homes of the Procurators of St. Mark

A DEFINITIVE ARCHITECTURAL AND TOWN LAYOUT OF THE PIAZZA SAN MARCO

Between 1469 and 1530 Mauro Codussi, Bartolomeo Bon and Guglielmo de' Grigi built the Procuratie Vecchie.
The fabric, originally only one storey high (the second was added later), has an uninterrupted series of fifty arches at groundfloor level and twice the number of windows on the upper floors.

Sansovino's ideas of constructional and urbanistic renewal of the Square, begun with the building of the Library, which created a new building line detached from the bell-tower, were taken up by Scamozzi who demolished the Orseolo Hospice, began the building of the Procuratie Nuove in 1587, continuing the traditional scheme of an arcaded ground floor.
On the death of the architect in 1616, the building had arrived at the tenth arch and from then was continued by Baldassare Longhena in 1634 who finally completed the building.

126

THE CORRER MUSEUM

THE PICTURE GALLERY AND THE HISTORIC COLLECTIONS OF VENETIAN LIFE

THE PRINT AND DRAWING ROOMS

THE LIBRARY

The Correr Museum has its seat in the rooms of the Procuratie Nuove with entry up the large stairway of the Ala Napoleonica. The museum is sub-divided in two parts; the first with collections regarding history and customs of Venice (paintings, prints, documents, costumes, ship models, coins, arms, flags, seals, sculpture); the second, the Quadreria is rich in many paintings, among the painters particular attention should be paid to Paolo and Lorenzo Veneziano, Jacobello del Fiore, Michele Giambono, the Vivarini, Vittore Carpaccio, Giovanni and Gentile Bellini, Antonello da Messina and Cosmè Tura.

127

128

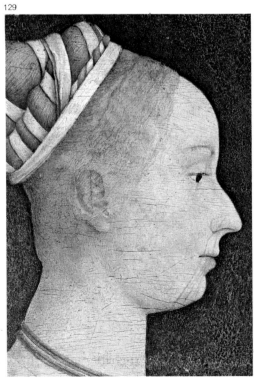

129

125 St. Mark's Square. Procuratie Nuove
126 « The two ladies », V. Carpaccio
     (Correr Museum)
127 « Portrait of a gentleman ». B. Estense
128 « Youth with a red cap », V. Carpaccio
129 « Portrait of an aristocratic lady »,
     A. Maccagnini

49

THE MARCIANA LIBRARY

JACOPO SANSOVINO

130

In the angle which the Piazzetta forms with the waterfront, from 1537 to 1545 the Mint was built to the plan of Jacopo Sansovino.
Here were minted the most famous Venetian coins, the golden ducat or sequin, a coin eagerly welcomed in all the markets of Europe and the Orient.
Now the building is used as a depository and reading room of the adjacent Marciana Library.
This last-named building was also built by Jacopo Sansovino, starting from 1537.
The works continued till 1554 and ended at the sixteenth of the arches.
In 1583 Vincenzo Scamozzi completed the fabric, turning the corner towards the Basin so that it met the Mint.
The Library consisted of the bequest of Cardinal Bessarion (1468), rich in precious illuminated incunabula, to which in time were added other valuable works.
The Vestibule was at one time the hall where lecturers in philosophy and letters held public lessons.
The ceiling, planned and built between 1550 and 1560 by Cristoforo Rosa, is enriched by a painting by Titian representing « Wisdom ».
The room houses valuable examples of Byzantine, Venetian and foreign bindings from the 10th to 13th Century.
From here one enters the huge Hall of the Library (26.50 x 10.70 m).

CARDINAL BESSARION'S LEGACY

In the cases are displayed the rarest books and manuscripts of the bequest of Cardinal Bessarion: illustrated editions of the 16th Century, among them the famous editions of Manuzio.
Hence the very famous « Grimani Breviary » of the end of the 15th Century, valuable for its 110 full page miniatures, illustrating the Calendar and episodes taken from the Old and New Testaments.

130 « The month of January »,
    Grimani Breviary
131 The Marciana Library, J. Sansovino
132 The Island of San Giorgio
133 The church of San Giorgio, interior
134 The cloister of the cypresses

131

132

THE ISLAND OF SAN GIORGIO

133

A VERY ANCIENT BENEDICTINE MONASTERY

A COMPLEX ARCHITECTURAL UNDERTAKING

St. George, in olden times called the Island of Cypresses, which grew here in abundance, was granted by the Republic in 982 to Giovanni Morosini who installed a Benedictine Monastery there, which, thanks to privileges, donations and bequests, developed so as to become very quickly a religious and cultural centre of European fame.

The buildings which used to stand on the island were destroyed in the earthquake of 1223 and rebuilt with financial aid from Doge Pietro Ziani. Starting in the first half of the 15th Century, there began that great work of building transformation of the monastery, which went on until the first years of the 17th Century. The architect Michelozzo Michelozzi, who Cosimo, Lord of Florence in exile in Padua had brought with him, built the Library, the first example in Venice of Renaissance architecture (unfortunately destroyed). The dormitory or « Manica lunga » with the cells of the brethren aligned along the 128 m. long central corridor is by Giovanni Buora. The Cloister of the Laurels to the plan of the same Buora, was, however executed by his son Andrea. From 1559 Andrea Palladio worked on the island, building the Refectory, between 1559 and 1563, the Church of St. George with the square in front of it, begun in 1579 and not finished till about 1610, and the Cloister of the Cypresses from 1579 until 1614.

In the 17th Century the last amendments were executed by Longhena: the large Stairway in the first cloister (1641-1643), the Apartment of the Abbots and the Library (1641-1671).

134

SAN MARCO

THE MOST DENSELY BUILT UP SESTIERE

135

Through the great archway of the Tower the alley of the Merceria leads into the Square. The alley, of very ancient origin, linked with the primitive formation of the city, connected the political religious centre of San Marco with the business centre, Rialto. The building design of the street, which at some points presents Gothic traces, was to a great extent transformed in the 16th Century and again in following times.
The Merceria, even to-day, is one of the most important and frequented streets in Venice; it is lined by an uninterrupted succession of elegant shops.

LE MERCERIE
THE SMART STREET OF SHOPS

THE FIRST IMPORTANT THOROUGHFARE FROM THE PIAZZA SAN MARCO TO SAN SALVADOR AND THE RIALTO

THE CLOCK TOWER

The Clock Tower is a Renaissance building, possibly to the design of Mauro Codussi, carried out at the end of the 15th Century; in the first decade of the 16th Century Pietro Lombardo added the two wings to the pre-existent central part of the Tower.
On the upper terrace has been placed the bell struck by two Moors, virile bronze figures.
The great clock has the indications of the phases of the moon and the movement of the sun in correspondence to the signs of the zodiac.

137

136

135   The Sestiere of San Marco
136   The « Mori »
137   The Clock Tower
138   Campo San Salvador
139   Tommaso Rangone on the façade of the church of San Zulian
140   The Church of San Salvador, interior

138

139

TOMMASO RANGONE ON THE FAÇADE OF
SAN ZULIAN

Of very ancient foundation it was rebuilt towards the middle of the 16th Century, it seems to the plan of J. Sansovino and A. Vittoria.
The building was constructed at the expense of a Ravenna doctor, Tommaso Rangone whose statue can be seen above the entrance portal.
It is one of the earliest examples where the façade of a Church has become a monument in celebration of a person.

TWO BAROQUE FAÇADES IN
CAMPO SAN SALVADOR

The foundation of the Church of S. Salvador seems to go back to the 7th Century.
Renewed in Gothic times it was newly rebuilt between 1507 and 1534 to the design of Antonio Spavento, then superseded by Tullio Lombardo. The façade was erected by G. Sardi in 1663.
The monastery, too, was completely rebuilt by Sansovino after 1534.

The plan is with three naves with three central domes where Scamozzi opened the lanterns in 1574 to obtain more light.
On the main altar, thought up by Guglielmo dei Grigi is a painting of Titian's mature years, to cover the silver-gilt altar-piece, an exquisite example of Venetian goldsmithery of the beginning of the 14th Century.

The Scuola (Fraternity) of St. Theodore which rises beside the church was one of the Great Scuole of the city of Venice.
The building was begun in 1580.
From 1608 to 1613 Tommaso Contin carried the work forward, arranging the workshops in the alley and building the great stairway.
Following a large bequest the façade was built between 1649 and 1655 to the design of G. Sardi.

140

GIORGIO SPAVENTO PLANNED THE CHURCH AND SARDI DID THE FAÇADE

FROM THE ACCADEMIA TO THE RIALTO

The wooden Accademia Bridge across the Grand Canal was built for the first time by the Austrians in the year 1854.

141

142

THE CHURCH OF SAN VIDAL

A FAÇADE BY TIRALI

The Church of San Vidal, which stands at the entrance to the Campo, was founded in the 11th Century. The present building is of the 17th Century to the design of Antonio Gaspari, while the façade was erected by Andrea Tirali at the beginning of the 18th Century.
Important paintings inside: « San Vitale on horseback with Saints » (Vittore Carpaccio), « The Immaculate Conception » (Sebastiano Ricci) and « The Angel Raphael and Saints » (ca. 1730) G. B. Piazzetta.

CAMPO SAN STEFANO

A GREAT SPACE FOR STROLLING AND RESTING

Campo Santo Stefano, one of the largest and most characteristic places in Venice, is still to-day very much frequented.
Here in olden times there were rich festivals in which numerous crowds of the ordinary people took part.
Here was held the last bull-fight in Venice in 1802. For some years there was a weekly market, formerly at St. Mark's Square.
At one time some of the houses round the Square had façades decorated in frescoes, the work of Jacopo Tintoretto and Giuseppe Salviati, and it would appear also by Giorgione.
In 18th Century prints it is possible to observe shops existing at that time, among them a chemist's shop still operating at the present time. It was the custom for Venetians to walk back and forth through the Square of Santo Stefano; this type of stroll was called « liston » because it took place along a paved strip of road, running through the middle of the Square longitudinally, while the rest of the space was still kept unpaved and covered with grass.
Along this paved strip there were also stone or wooden seats, so that one might sit down and rest awhile between one stroll and another.
The favourite hour was that towards sunset, but during the summer season there were those people who enjoyed taking the air in the early hours of evening.
Facing the Church, the building now transformed into a restaurant was the seat of the Scuola of the Laneri, manufacturers and weavers of woollen cloth.

143

141 San Vidal, campanile
142 The church of Santo Stefano
143 The entrance to Campo Santo Stefano
144 The Pisani Palace
145 The Morosini Palace
146 The church of San Vidal and the Loredan Palace

144

THE PALAZZO PISANI

Now the seat of the Conservatory of
Music, named after the famous
musician of Venice, Benedetto
Marcello.
The building began at the beginning
of the 17th Century to the design of
Bartolomeo Monopola and was
completed by Frigimelica who
heightened it and created open
loggias in the courtyard.
The interior rooms are decorated
with stuccoes, gilding and frescoes
by painters of the 18th Century,
such as Guarana, Amigoni, Ricci,
Domenico Tiepolo and Pittoni.
The collection of antique musical
instruments (of particular value, a
Stradivarius and an Amati) was
the property of the Hospice of the
Pietà.

145

THE PALAZZO
MOROSINI

It is a building of the 17th Century
once belonging to Doge Francesco
Morosini, the Peloponnesiac (thus
nicknamed for his victories in the
East against the Turks, the last in
the history of Venice, and for
re-conquering Morea).

THE PALAZZO
LOREDAN

Isolated between the Square
and the rio of San Vidal, the Loredan
Palace was rebuilt on a Gothic
fabric by Antonio Scarpagnino
(16th Century).
It is now the seat of the Veneto
Institute of Science, Letters
and Arts.

146

THE GOTHIC DOORWAY AND THE WOODEN CEILING OF THE

CHURCH OF SAN STEFANO

At the end of the Campo, the side of the Church of Santo Stefano closes the area.
The present building, which goes back to the 14th Century (finished in 1374), is of a conventual type in three naves.
The façade was enriched in the first half of the 15th Century by Bartolomeo Bon's decorated architrave.
The wooden ship's keel roof of the nave and the decorations are of the same period.
In the Sacristy are three great canvases by Tintoretto with episodes from the Life of Christ.

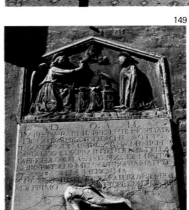

A SHOE THE EMBLEM OF THE CALEGHERI

Before being transferred to the Campo of San Tomà, it seems that the Scuola of the Calegheri (shoemakers) had its seat here. The emblem of a shoe appears on the 14th Century pilasters and on the plate built into the wall on high.

THE HOUSE OF VERONESE IN SALIZZADA SAN SAMUELE
THE FORMER THEATRE OF SAN SAMUELE

In this house, the windows of which are decorated with Renaissance reliefs, Paolo Veronese lived for a time, and died 1588.

In the calle del Teatro, where now stands a modern school, there used to be the celebrated old theatre of San Samuele, built in the first place in 1655 for the Grimanis, and re-built in 1747. On this stage were to be seen the most famous actors and the most celebrated masques of the period; Carlo Goldoni staged many of his plays in this place.

147 The church of Santo Stefano, the wooden ceilling
148 Paolo Veronese's house
149 The Emblem of the Scuola dei Calegheri (shoemakers)
150 Campo Sant'Angelo
151 The Magno Palace, doorway
152 The Minelli Palace, spiral stairway
153 The Gritti Palace

151

THE GOTHIC DOORWAY OF
THE PALAZZO MAGNO

In the calle della Vida rises the Contarini del Bovolo Palace, a Gothic building.
Its name derives from the existence in the little campo behind of a charming and original spiral staircase (bovolo) erected between the end of the 15th and the beginning of the 16th Century; it has a series of arches with parapet and small columns which follow the rising line of the stair.

152

THE CHARACTERISTIC SPIRAL STAIRCASE OF THE
PALAZZO MINELLI AT SAN LUCA

153

CAMPO SANT'ANGELO

A DESTROYED CHURCH AND
A ROW OF POINTED-ARCH
PALACES

Campo Sant'Angelo: where in olden days stood the Church of the same name which was demolished in 1837. From the campo can be seen the Gothic bell-tower of Santo Stefano leaning noticeably.
Certain interesting mansions are to be seen around this campo, Palazzo Gritti and Palazzo Duodo (registered numbers 3822 and 3584) both in Gothic style; Palazzo Pisani of the 17th Century.
At the end of the 18th Century Palazzo Duodo was used as a hotel with the sign of the Three Stars; in 1801, after having lived there for several years, the celebrated maestro and composer, Domenico Cimarosa, author, among other compositions of the opera « Il Matrimonio Segreto », died there.

CAMPO SAN FANTIN

THE CHURCH, THE SCUOLA OF SAN GIROLAMO AND THE FENICE THEATRE

The Church, erected at the beginning of the 16th Century to the design of Scarpagnino, was finished in 1564 by Sansovino in the part of the apse. The Scuola, known also as that of the Picai or of the Buona Morte (Good Death) since the confraternity had the pitiful duty of accompanying those condemned to death to the scene of execution, rose between the end of the 16th and beginning of the 17th Century to the design of Antonio Contin and Alessandro Vittoria.

The theatre was always an important social institution in Venice and one of its major attractions. Nearly all the numerous theatre halls at one time existent in Venice have been demolished.

The « La Fenice » Theatre was inaugurated as recently as 1792, not many years before the fall of the Republic which had entrusted G. Antonio Selva with its construction.

A fire, however, destroyed it almost completely in the year 1836, but it was immediately re-built by the Meduna brothers who tried, as far as possible, to preserve the original late 18th Century taste of the rich decoration of gilded carvings and sculpture in wood and stucco in the huge oval hall capable of accommodating 1,500 seats.

FROM SAN STEFANO TO SAN MARCO THROUGH
CAMPO SAN MAURIZIO CAMPO DEL GIGLIO AND SAN MOISÈ

Next to the 19th Century Church stands the 16th Century Bellavite palace, whose owner, so that he might have the ancient bell tower demolished, engaged to pay to the friars of San Maurizio a heavy annual tax.
Alessandro Manzoni lived there in the year 1803.
Facing it is the rich Zaguri Palace a building of the first half of the 15th Century.
In the calle del Doge is the Da Ponte Palace built by Doge Nicolò (second half of 16th Century).

THE BELLAVITE PALACE: A tax for demolishing the campanile

TWO FAÇADES FOR THE BARBARO FAMILY AND FOR THE FINI FAMILY
SAN MOISÈ   SANTA MARIA DEL GIGLIO

Founded in the 9th Century, it was re-built later. The rich façade was completed by Giuseppe Sardi between 1678 and 1683.
In the first order on the plinths of the stylobate, is a series of plans in relief of cities and fortresses linked with the political career of members of the Barbaro family who commissioned the façade (Zara, Candia, Padua, Rome, Corfù, Split).

Of extremely old foundation, possibly of the 8th Century, the Church of San Moisè underwent its first rebuilding in the 13th Century, of which remains to-day nothing but the fine bell tower.
The works on the present fabric were begun in 1632.
In 1668 Alessandro Tremignon began the façade, singular in the richness and superabundance of its plastic decorations in high relief.

THE WORKING CLASS SESTIERE OF CASTELLO

On the series of islands which now form the sestiere di Castello, it seems that there arose the first inhabitable settlements of the city, even in the centuries preceding 810 the year in which the government moved from Malamocco to Rivoaltus. The name of the district comes from the existence of a very ancient castle built for the defence of the Rialto islands and guarding the nearby port of San Nicoiò. From this castle then went the other defensive system of the islands consisting of a line of walls which went as far up as the present

campo of Santa Maria Zobenigo, where à huge, heavy iron chain barred, should the necesssity have arisen, the passage of the Grand Canal.
The end island was also called in the early days « Olivolo » because of its shape, which seemed similar to that of an olive, or because of the presence of olive trees.
On this island in 774 a new bishopric had its seat, known first as Olivolo, then later as Castello.
Once the patriarchate of Grado was suppressed in 1451, the bishop of Castello assumed the title of Patriarch of Venice.

160

THE SEAT OF THE PRIMICERIO, THE BISHOP OF ST. MARK

SANT'APOLLONIA

The Church of the Saints Filippo e Giacomo was completely demolished at the beginning of the 19th Century. The only thing saved from destruction was the beautiful cloister of St. Apollonia, which can be reached along the short fondamenta at the foot of the Canonica bridge.
The cloister, the only example of Romanesque architecture remaining in Venice, was erected between the 12th and 13th Centuries. The original structure has come down to

us exactly as it was, in spite of the fact that it was disfigured by 17th Century heightenings.
On an almost square plan, the cloister is expressed architectonically by semicircular arches in brickwork with double lintels, supported by single and twin columns alternating around the four sides.
In 1472 the monastery of St. Apollonia, because of its proximity to the ducal basilica, was placed under the jurisdiction of the chief dignitary of St. Mark's, a prerogative which it maintained until the fall of the Republic.
This dignitary ranked equal with a bishop and was nominated by the Venetian senate among the noble clergy of the city for the care of the basilica of St. Mark, and depended directly on the doge and on the procurators.

THE VERY BEAUTIFUL ROMANESQUE CLOISTER

THE RIVA DEGLI SCHIAVONI

The Riva degli Schiavoni was thus
called because the Dalmatians were
wont to land there; it was enlarged
in 1780 from the Ponte della Paglia
as far as Ponte della Pietà and later
as far as the Napoleonic Gardens.
The fondamenta was paved in brick
for the first time in the year 1324;
along the way, partly on land, partly
in the water, the Dalmatians or
« Schiavoni » had here their places
for boats and shops.
Near the Riva degli Schiavoni during
a rising in 1172, the Doge Vitale
II Michiel was done to death by
the insurrectionists.

161

162

A FOREIGN COMMUNITY IN VENICE: THE GREEKS

AN ORGANIZED SOCIAL AND CULTURAL NUCLEUS

163

THE CHURCH OF SAN GIORGIO AND THE FLANGINI COLLEGE
SANTE LOMBARDO AND BALDASSARE LONGHENA

The Rio dei Greci was so-called
from the Greek community which
used to live here and who still to-day
have along the rio their Church of
San Giorgio, a Renaissance work
by Sante Lombardo, the Scuola di
San Nicolò and the Flangini College
from the name of the founder, built
by Longhena towards 1678.
The somewhat sloping, slender bell
tower of the Church, serves as a
landmark.
Nearer to the Ponte della Pietà
on the right are the two palaces
Cappello-Memmo and Gritti, one in
Gothic style, the other Renaissance
of the early 16th Century.

160 The Cloister of Sant'Apollonia
161 The Riva degli Schiavoni
162 The Rio dei Greci
163 The church of San Giorgio dei Greci

SAN ZACCARIA

The religious complex, church and monastery, was one of the most important in the city.

The foundation was due to the Doge Giustiniano Partecipazio (827-829). Every year, by tradition, right from the earliest times, the Doge with the Signoria went in great pomp to San Zaccaria, to visit the convent of the nuns, who used nearly all to belong to noble families.

Between the end of the 9th and the first half of the 10th Century came the first re-building of the church, of which only the crypt remains to-day.

In the 13th and in the first half of the 14th Century, the fabric underwent fresh changes. Of this period remain the bell tower, and the apsidal portion, known as the Chapel of San Tarasio, in Gothic style.

The left lateral nave of this building was, in the 15th Century incorporated in the new Church which we see to-day and which Antonio Gambello began to build in 1458 from the apsidal part.

In 1480 the first architect who was working on Gothic lines was joined by Mauro Codussi who completed the building of the nave and the new façade.

In the interior the grafting is clearly visible between the Gothic elements of the apsidal part and the presbytery with the Renaissance nave. Inside the church are paintings by J. Palma the Y. and an altar piece by Giovanni Bellini, « The Virgin and Child enthroned », a signed work dated 1505.

GOTHIC
AND RENAISSANCE

THE OLD CHURCH AND THE NEW CHURCH

VITTORE GAMBELLO

MAURO CODUSSI

167

THE POLYPTYCH OF SANTA SABINA: A MASTERPIECE OF THE FIFTEENTH CENTURY

In the Chapel of St. Tarasio there is a large polyptych « Santa Sabina » by Giovanni and Antonio da Murano, carved and gilded according to the flamboyant Gothic style.

166

164 The church of San Zaccaria
165 The Convent of San Zaccaria, the great cloister
166 The church of San Zaccaria, interior
167 Polyptych of Santa Sabina (San Zaccaria)
168 Rio dell'Osmarin
169 The Priuli Palace

169

THE PALAZZO PRIULI

The nearby Calle degli Albanesi took its name from the community of foreigners living there and carrying on commercial activities. Along the Canale dell'Osmarin stands the grandiose Priuli Palace, erected in the first half of the 15th Century by Giovanni Priuli who died here in 1456. It is a very beautiful building in flamboyant Gothic style with a many-mullioned window on the main floor and elegant corner windows.

168

170

THE HOSPICE OF THE PIETÀ

A SOCIAL WELFARE INITIATIVE FOR JUVENILES FOUNDED BY THE REPUBLIC

171

The Hospice of the Pietà, founded in 1346 and first known as a Foundling Hospital, had various seats till it found a fixed dwelling place in this part of the city; in time it assumed a more precise social function, that of providing for the maintenance and musical education of young orphans.

The concerts that these young artists used to give publicly in the church were famous in this and other similar Institutes.

The Hall of the church was transformed into an auditorium and was crowded to the doors by a Venetian and foreign public.

The Hospice of the Pietà is further celebrated for having had as « Choirmaster », for nearly 40 years, the Venetian musician Antonio Vivaldi, known as the Red Priest from the colour of his hair.

The Church was built to the plan of Giorgio Massari between 1745 and 1760; the Hospice, on the other hand, was never completed.

A MUSICAL PAST

ANTONIO VIVALDI

A CONCERT HALL

THE NAVE OF THE CHURCH

172

173

174

THE SCHOOL OF
SAN GIORGIO DEGLI SCHIAVONI
AND THE SERIES OF PAINTINGS BY VITTORE CARPACCIO

THE LIVES OF ST. GEORGE, ST. TRIFONE, ST. JEROME, THE PATRON SAINTS OF THE DALMATIANS

The Scuola of San Giorgio stands near Sant'Antonin at the end of the fondamenta dei Furlani, so-called because the area used to be inhabited by citizens who had come from Friuli.
The building was erected at the beginning of the 16th Century.
The interior is still visited because it preserves a valuable cycle of paintings by Vittore Carpaccio, executed between 1502 and 1509 with stories of the three Dalmatian saints: « Episodes in the life of St. George » (killing of the dragon; triumph of the saint; Baptism of the King and Queen of Libya), « Episodes in the life of St. Trifone of Bithynia », « Life of St. Jerome, Bishop of Split », (the tamed lion, the saint in his study, the funeral of St. Jerome), and other paintings of the Life of Christ.

175

THE " CAMPO " AND THE CHURCH OF SAN GIOVANNI IN BRAGORA

A peaceful, sunny Venetian square with the little Gothic church founded in the 9th Century, and re-built towards 1475.
The Gritti Badoer Palace is an edifice which retains, in spite of successive alterations the asymmetrical Gothic façade of the 15th Century.
Beside the Palace is the calle della Morte, whose denomination derives from a tradition or legend according to which those condemned to death by the Court of the Council of Ten were brought here and executed by night.

176

THE ARSENAL

Ten thousand ship-builders employed in the construction and repairing of dromons, galleys, skiffs, merchant ships, tartans, galliots, galleasses, feluccas, trading vessels, frigates, brigs, two-master sailing ships, bilanders.

Along the fondamenta della Tana on one side or from the Riva degli Schiavoni on the other, one arrives in front of the entrance to the Arsenal, a great basin of water, surrounded by walls where from the most ancient times the boats of the military or commercial fleets of the Republic were built.

The complex was one of the most vital centres of the city, linked with the type of economy on which was based the fortune of Venice.

This accounts for the great care always bestowed by the authority in charge of this, in overseeing and in making available all the means to ensure that the Arsenal was always at the highest point of efficiency. The craftsmen engaged in the work, who in the period of greatest splendour amounted to 15,000 units, were known as the « arsenalotti » and enjoyed special privileges and a special treatment from an economic point of view, in comparison with other categories of workers and artisans.

They also came here to accomplish all the other activities connected with navigation, such as the manufacture of riggings, of oakum, of sails and all naval equipment. Tradition has it that the Arsenal was founded in 1104; with the passage of time it grew larger with more capacious graving docks and huger sheds.

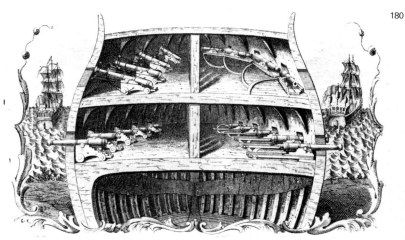

177 The walls of the Arsenal
178 « The Bucentaur », F. Guardi
179 « The cannonball store in the Arsenal » (Correr Museum)
180 « Section of a warship » (Correr Museum)

The building of the Casa del Canevo, or « della Tana » goes back to 1325, and was re-built in 1579 by Antonio da Ponte, 300 metres long, and subdivided into three corridors, it was here they used to make the riggings.

This long room was called « Tana » from the name of the town on the banks of the River Don from which the Venetians used to import the crude hemp. The « Visdomini del Canevo » (or « della Tana »), the magistrates attached to this sphere of activity, had their offices in the square. The entrance portal dates back to 1460 and was designed by Antonio Gambello, and might well have been one of the earliest in Venetian Renaissance style.

Around 1547 the shed of the Bucentaur was built. This housed the huge Venetian ceremonial galley, several decks in height, furnished with two hundred oars, decorated in gold with wood carvings depicting mythological and symbolical figures, and with a high prow which was occupied by the Doge and the Signoria, during the most important of the many ceremonies in the Venetian year: « The Marriage of the Sea » which took place near San Nicolò at Lido, at which the Doge, casting a gold ring into the sea, reaffirmed the special link between the city and the sea.

181 « Italy » (Doge's Palace)
182 The doorway to the Arsenal
183 « A Sea Captain » (Correr Museum)
184 « War fleet in siege formation » (Correr Museum)

182

183

184

THE NAVAL MUSEUM

A HISTORICAL PICTURE OF
THE VENETIANS
AT SEA

SHIPS AND SEA CAPTAINS,
BATTLES, CONQUESTS,
COMMERCIAL TREATIES

185

186

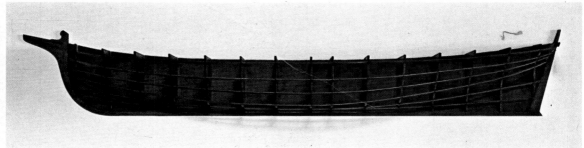

187

At present, the Naval Museum,
along the Riva dei Sette Martiri,
is housed in what was once a
granary of the Republic.
The Museum has a collection of
standards, adornments and
embellishments of ships, small models
of ancient ships and of the last
Bucentaur, paintings representing
scenes of battle, portraits of great
men of the sea, and so on.
In addition to such mementos, it
has log-books, maps, nautical
instruments, and in particular the
portolan chart of Europe and
N. Africa of Diego Homen,
Portuguese.

185 « Ships leaving from the Basin » (Naval Museum)
186 A section of a ship (Naval Museum)
187 A fishing boat (Naval Museum)
188 An iron gondola prow (Correr Museum)
189 Gondolas in the Bacino Orseolo
190 Design for a gondola

188

A WHOLLY
VENETIAN BOAT

THE GONDOLA

189

The gondola, the so characteristic lagoon craft, can be reckoned among the symbols of the city.

The gondola was mentioned for the first time in a document dated 1094. During the centuries it has undergone certain changes in its shape while managing to retain its own special characteristics.

Compared with its present-day form, better balanced and responsive with poop and prow arching upwards, raised above the water, the gondola of the 15th and 16th Centuries, as can be observed in numerous paintings, had a more horizontal and much lower line.

It was from the 18th Century that the craft assumed its classic and better-known form, 11.50 metres long and 1.40 metres wide.

The construction of a gondola is a toilsome business and calls for specialists to shape the almost 280 pieces of which it is composed, consisting of numerous different kinds of wood.

The gondola is usually steered by an oarsman (who preserves his equilibrium by his handling of the long oar) standing on the poop, but it does happen at times that there are a couple of oarsmen.

The prow is decorated with a curious toothed iron ornament, and at the poop is another in volute shape; both were often richly and fantastically elaborated by the old-time craftsmen, but, however rich the decoration, the basic design remained the same. Different again were the embellishments of the gondola, such as the sea horses on each side of the seat, the wooden surfaces forming the cover of the prow, carved in floral motives and gilded, and finally the small cabin, a kind of little kiosk, situated in the middle of the boat, with tiny windows hung with black felt curtains with tassels and cords.

How many gondolas there were in the centuries of the Republic's greatest splendour is not known, but even in the 18th Century there were more than 10,000; to-day there are no more than 500 at the tourist's disposition.

To make a comparison with modern days, the gondola used to be for the Venetian what the motor-car is for the townsman of to-day; a private means of transport along the canals of the city.

190

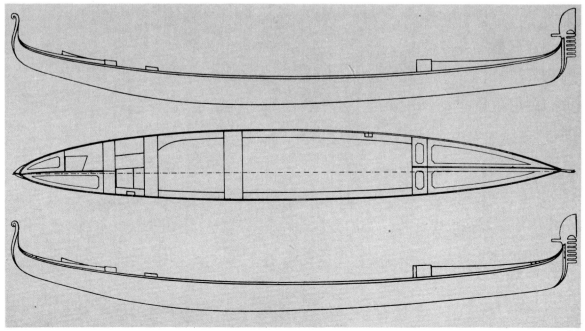

CALLI, SMALL SQUARES, CANALS AT CASTELLO

Brief traces of the old town and the purely humble life
with a flavour of bygone times can be found

191

192

193

194

195

196

CAMPO DI RUGA
CALLE DI RUGA
FONDAMENTA RIELLO
FONDAMENTA DELLA TANA
CORTE NUOVA
CALLE DI SAN GIOACCHINO
CALLE LARGA
SALIZZADA STRETTA
CORTE SOLDÀ
CORTE CORRERA

Campo and calle di Ruga, so-called from the houses and shops along these streets. The two small palaces of the 16th and 17th Century, seen on the longest side are certainly very interesting.
The fondamenta della Tana takes its name from the building previously referred to, where at one time ropes for the ships used to be made.
Corte Nuova is a characteristic small Venetian Campiello, rectangular in form, flanked by rows of modest apartment houses, built by public or private enterprise. Two well-heads characterize the campiello, in which there was at one time, and is still to-day, though to a lesser degree, an extremely busy community life, and in addition, considerable activity in the various crafts and trades.
Corte Soldà derives its name from a Venetian family who used to live there. An Alvise Soldà or Solta, a ship-owner, in the year 1560 built a house for his family, which, according to the records of the Council of Ten in 1566, consisted of twenty persons. The façade is characterized by a four-mullioned window with balcony.

The present Via Garibaldi was obtained by covering over the rio di Castello on the initiative of the Napoleonic administration; at that time it was called Via Eugenia and constituted the first part of a plan fortunately never realized, which envisaged the joining of Venice to the mainland going across Sant'Erasmo and le Vignole, by means of a series of roads and bridges.
This street, in the middle of the thickly-populated quarter of Castello, seat of a market, is extremely colourful.

THE ANCIENT RIO OF CASTELLO FILLED IN: VIA GARIBALDI

THE BUSY ATMOSPHERE OF A LOCAL MARKET: VEGETABLES AND FISH

THE HOUSE OF THE CABOT FAMILY

A family of celebrated navigators, the father, Giovanni, set sail in 1497 from England under orders from Henry VII to repeat what Columbus had done; the son, Sebastiano, born, possibly in Venice in 1476 or 1477, took part with his father in the voyage to Canada. Later, he undertook a considerable number of voyages, on behalf now of England, now of Spain.

SAN PIETRO DI CASTELLO

THE ANCIENT PALACE OF THE PATRIARCH OF VENICE

A PALLADIAN CHURCH

The first Venetian episcopal seat was instituted in Olivolo in 775.
One reads that in 841 a church dedicated to St. Peter was erected in place of an older one.
Following a fire, the building was restored, and in fact re-built in the 12th Century. In 1556 the patriarchal seat was occupied by Antonio Diedo who had the idea of renewing the entire complex of St. Peter. With this in mind, he engaged Andrea Palladio who carried out a project of complete reconstruction.
Very shortly after the work had been begun, it was interrupted by the death of the Patriarch; only at the end of the 16th Century did Lorenzo Priuli take up once again the initiative of Diedo, and Smeraldi, the architect, was put in charge of the work. The artist completed the façade in accordance with the Palladian models between 1594 and 1596.
But work was carried on, too, to the body of the church, which was also re-built from 1619 onwards, under the direction of the architect Girolamo Grapiglia.
The stupendous main altar was erected in 1649 by Clemente Moli to a design by Longhena.
It was that same Longhena who designed the Chapel in honour of Cardinal Francesco Vendramin. The lateral cloister, seat of the patriarch, was renewed.

THE CAMPANILE BY MAURO CODUSSI

The bell-tower, which stands isolated in the square, is the work of Mauro Codussi, at the end of the 15th Century. It is an interesting Renaissance work, the only bell-tower in Venice panelled with slabs of worked Istrian stone and topped by an elegant bell chamber.

203

204

AN ANCIENT TOWN LAYOUT HOARY WITH CENTURIES AND HISTORY WHICH STILL EXISTS AND LIVES

CAMPO DELLE GATTE
PONTE DEGLI SCUDI
THE ZENO VENIER PALACE
CALLE DEL MANDOLIN
CAMPO DUE POZZI
CALLE MAGNO
CALLE DONÀ
PONTE DELLA SCOAZZERA
THE DONÀ PALACE
CAMPO SANTA TERNITA
CAMPO DELLA CELESTIA
CALLE DEL CIMITERO

205

Campo delle Gatte, which derives its name from the presence on this site of the Legati (Legates) or apostolic nuncios, before being transferred to San Francesco della Vigna.
In one of the houses in this square between 1792 and 1796 lived Ugo Foscolo, while still young, with his mother and brothers.
From Ponte degli Scudi along the rio can be seen the Gothic Zeno-Venier 15th Century Palace.
The campo Due Pozzi is characterized by working-class dwellings.
In calle Donà stands the palace of the same name, the façade of which is better seen from the Scoazzera bridge.
The bridge was thus called because of its nearness to a « scoazzera », that is to say, a large vessel in which was put the street refuse which was later carried away by boatmen, in special barges, to somewhere outside the city.

THE CHURCH OF SAN MARTINO

Founded in the 8th Century, the church of San Martino, after various re-buildings, was completely re-constructed to the design of Jacopo Sansovino towards the middle of the 16th Century. The interior was decorated with frescoes and stuccoes in the 18th Century by Domenico Bruni, Jacopo Guarana and Fabio Canal.

Certain Gothic style houses could date from the 14th Century.
Of the old houses of the Magno family, apart from the great ogival portal with remains of the 15th Century wooden door, the Gothic façade, and, inside, the courtyard with an external stairway remain.
In the first years of the 16th Century, the historiographer, Stefano Magno lived here, author of a well-known and extremely interesting « Venetian Chronicle ».
The church of Santa Ternita, which had been in existence since the 11th Century in the square of the same name, was demolished in 1832 and in its place was built a dwelling house; the bell-tower which rose isolated in the middle of the square, fell unexpectedly in 1880. Near the church in the 16th Century there used to be the printing establishment of the celebrated engraver, Francesco Marcolini, of Forlì.
The friendship between Marcolini and Pietro Aretino is well-known.
Chronicles of the time refer to a too-warm friendship between Aretino and the wife of Marcolini, which led to the break-up of relations.

Campo della Celestia is the vulgarization of Santa Maria Celeste to which the church, now no longer in existence, was dedicated.
On the other hand, though in a very bad condition, there remains the cloister of the nuns' convent founded at the end of the 12th Century.
Sanudo, in his diary, mentions that « in the year 1509 the nuns of the Celestia danced the whole night through with certain young patricians to the sound of fifes and trumpets, and that the Patriarch having gone to reprove them for their conduct, seized one, of the Tagliapietra family, and cut off her braids, but then, wishing to imprison two others outside the convent, the nuns all crowded tumultuously at the door and forced him to desist » (Tassini).

SAN FRANCESCO DELLA VIGNA

A QUESTION OF HARMONIOUS PROPORTIONS APPLIED TO ARCHITECTURE

The Church of San Francesco della Vigna, together with the convent, was founded in the 12th Century. It was rebuilt in Gothic times between the 14th and 15th Centuries. From this period remain the three lovely cloisters at the edge of the lagoon. The church, on the other hand, was re-built a second time by Sansovino between 1534 and 1568, and terminated as regards the façade by Andrea Palladio, 1568-1572.
The interior consists of a single nave with deep chapels along the longer sides. Among the paintings decorating the altars and the walls of the choir are works by J. Palma the Y., Andrea Vicentino, Francesco Maggiotto and Tintoretto.
On the altar of the Chapel of the Conception is « The Virgin and Child among saints », by Giovanni Bellini, a work signed and dated 1507. In the sacristy, « The sacred conversation » by Paolo Veronese.

THE FAÇADE IS BY PALLADIO

THE REPUBLIC PRESENTS A PALACE TO THE POPE DESTINED TO BE THE SEAT OF THE NUNCIOS

Facing the Church rises the Renaissance palace of the Nunziata, so-called because of being the seat of the Apostolic Nuncios, who lived formerly in Campo delle Gatte. The building was in fact, acquired by the Republic, and donated to Pope Pius IV in the year 1564.

206 The church of S. Francesco della Vigna
207 San Francesco della Vigna, cloister
208 The Palace of the Nuncios
209 The church of San Giovanni e Paolo

209

SAINTS JOHN AND PAUL

THE CHURCH AND THE CONVENT OF THE DOMINICANS

A RELIGIOUS INSTITUTION

The Church and the convent of the Saints Giovanni e Paolo rose on an area granted by the Republic to the Order of the Dominican Friars who began the building of the complex in the 13th Century.
The works continued over a good two centuries and began at the part of the apses, which, together with the transept, were finished towards 1368. Work continued then towards the façade and came to an end in 1430, the year of the consecration.
The interior has three naves, in the form of an Egyptian cross, with five apsidal chapels, and gives the same impression of magnificence as the church of Santa Maria dei Frari, emphasized in this case by the great luminosity resultant on the apses facing south.
The Church used to rank immediately after that of St. Mark for importance. Several Doges have been buried here in grandiose and architectonically important sepulchral monuments.

THE SCUOLA GRANDE OF SAN MARCO

A LAY INSTITUTION

Beside the church is the Scuola Grande di San Marco, instituted in 1260 with the name of the « Battuti ». The first seat having been destroyed, work on the present edifice began in 1487 to the design of Pietro Lombardo in collaboration with his son Tullio and Antonio Buora.
Three years later, in 1490, Lombardo was dismissed by the donors and the work was entrusted to Mauro Codussi, who completed the façade with the typical curvilinear crowning. In 1495 the fabric was complete but it was later amplified in the rear portion by Sansovino.
The Sala dell'Albergo (Hall of the Inn) on the first floor is interesting. It still preserves the inlaid wooden ceiling in blue and gold, the work of Biasio and Pietro da Faenza, 1504.

THE HOSPITAL OF THE MENDICANTI

A SOCIAL ASSISTANCE INSTITUTION

The buildings of the Ospedale dei Mendicanti (Beggars' Hospital) extend the whole length of the rio of the same name from the rear of the Scuola as far as the Fondamenta Nuove, around two arcaded cloisters.
In the centre of the group, tucked in between the two wings of the Hospice, is the Church, dedicated to San Lazzaro, designed by Vincenzo Scamozzi.
In 1636 both the Hospice and the Church were finished; the latter stands back from the waterfront, preceded by a great entrance hall, so that the execution of concerts should not be disturbed by noises coming from the street.
This Hospice, too, housed poor young girls and was a much appreciated Conservatory of Music. The external façade was erected later, in 1673, by G. Sardi (possibly to a design by the same Scamozzi), who also designed the grandiose funeral monument (which divides the nave from the vestibule) of Alvise Mocenigo, Procurator of San Marco, who defended Candia against the Turks, dying there in 1654.

Inside the Church of San Giovanni e Paolo, above the entrance door, is the monument to the Doge Pietro Mocenigo (who died in 1476) by Pietro Lombardo; it represents one of the most significant works of the Renaissance, in which the validity of the structural part corresponds well with an important moment in the plastic art of Venice.
In the right-hand nave, on the second altar is a valuable « Polyptych » by Bellini, executed around 1465.
In the transept, « Christ bearing the Cross » by Alvise Vivarini; on the next altar a painting by Lorenzo Lotto, « The alms-giving of St. Antoninus » (dated 1542).
At the head of the transept is a huge window in flamboyant Gothic style with 15th Century glass.
It is Murano work with enamels and stained glass (figures of saints, evangelists and doctors of the church and prophets) possibly carried out to a cartoon by Bartolomeo Vivarini.
In the presbytery are various monuments; one on the wall in Gothic style to Doge Michele Morosini (died 1382); to Doge Andrea Vendramin, one of the most significant works of the Renaissance attributed to Lombardo.
At one time the statues of Adam and Eve also figured in this monument, but they were removed and sold, because they were judged unsuitable for a holy place because of their nakedness. On the end wall of the transept on the left, is the monument to the Doge Sebastiano Venier, the one who won the Battle of Lepanto.
The cloisters of the convent are of the 16th and 17th Centuries, coming from a re-building of the pre-existent edifices in Gothic style, a rebuilding in which Longhena, too, took part.

210 SS. Giovanni e Paolo, great transept window
211 Scuola di San Marco, bas-relief on the façade
212 Scuola di San Marco at SS. Giovanni e Paolo

210
211

212

BARTOLOMEO COLLEONI

A MERCENARY COMMANDER OF THE REPUBLIC OF VENICE

The equestrian statue was erected in 1488 to a model by Andrea Verrocchio and Alessandro Leopardi proceeded with the casting and worked out the design of the plinth.

213

214

AN EXTREMELY BEAUTIFUL RENAISSANCE BUILDING

A small, but precious Renaissance building, the work of Pietro Lombardo, executed between 1481 and 1489.
Among the religious buildings of the Renaissance, it is one of the most representative, a complete and unitary expression of a new language.
The church has remained unaltered by any later intervention, something that happens so often in Venice. The walls, both inside and out are completely panelled with slabs of polychrome marble, with decorative inlays and smooth stripes which serve to create architectonic compartments.
The interior is in a single nave; the presbytery, which is reached by a central flight of steps, is raised above the floor of the church to make room for the crypt beneath.

THE CHURCH OF THE MIRACOLI

215

217

216

213, 214 Monument to Bartolomeo Colleoni
215 Santa Maria dei Miracoli, façade
216 The church of the Miracoli, side on canal
217 The church of the Miracoli, apse

SANTA MARIA FORMOSA

THE FESTIVAL OF THE SEVEN MARYS

218

219

The Church of Santa Maria Formosa seems to have been founded in the 8th Century. The edifice has been rebuilt several times, lastly beginning in 1491 by Mauro Codussi.
The building, however, was interrupted and only in 1542 was the façade towards the rio erected, and in 1604 the one towards the campo.
A unique example in Venice for its shape and its architectonic solutions, is seen in the bell chamber and the point of the bell-tower,
executed to the design of the priest Francesco Zuccoli between 1611 and the year 1688.
The key of the arch over the little entrance door to the bell-tower is extremely amusing with its motive of a grotesque mask.

The façades of the palaces which give shape to the spacious and irregular campo presenting the successive evolution of the most important moments in Venetian architecture.

220

Along the sides of the campo stand various palaces of varying periods: the Vitturi palace, Byzantine of the 12th Century, later modified but still preserving the original many-mullioned windows; the two Donà palaces of the 15th Century in Gothic style; along the shorter side the Priuli Ruzzini Palace of the 16th Century with the façade on the square re-built at the end of the century by Bartolomeo Monopola. On the opposite side on the rio characterized by the great number of bridges giving direct access to the houses, the Malipiero Trevisan Palace, built in the first years of the 16th Century to the design of Sante Lombardo.

218 The area round Santa Maria Formosa
219 A grotesque head on the campanile (S. Maria Formosa)
220 Campo Santa Maria Formosa
221 Campiello Querini
222 « Entrance of the Procurator into San Salvador », G. Bella (Querini Gallery)
223 Rio del Paradiso

In the Chapel of the Conception, the first on the right-hand nave, a triptych by Bartolomeo Vivarini, signed and dated 1473: « The Madonna of Mercy ».
Next comes « la Pietà » by J. Palma the Y., and « The Last Supper » by J. Bassano.
Then the Chapel of the School of the Bombardieri, the makers of mortars, where is to be seen the celebrated painting by J. Palma the E., representing « Santa Barbara » protectress of the school; the Chapel of the Scuola of the Casselleri, who used to make trunks for wedding trousseaux.
The Scuola had the privilege of being visited by the Doge every year on the day of the Festival of the Marys, a reminder of the help given by the trunk-makers on the occasion of the kidnapping by the Dalmatian pirates in 944, of young Venetian women, while they were celebrating a ceremony in the Church of S. Pietro di Castello.
The trunk-makers realized what had happened, chased the pirates and freed the young women.

221

A MODERN LIBRARY AND PICTURE GALLERY IN THE
QUERINI STAMPALIA PALACE

Going around the apses of the church, one arrives in the campiello Querini, from the name of the family who built the palace facing the rio at the beginning of the 16th Century. This building is now the seat of the Querini Stampalia Library. Here, too, is housed a Picture Gallery with many works, among them particularly, 69 paintings by Gabriele Bella of the middle of the 18th Cent. of great iconographic interest because of the subjects, all scenes of public life in Venice, many outside in the city, some inside the rooms of the Ducal Palace where it is possible to see the various magistracies meeting together, and the furnishing of the rooms.

222

223

CALLE DEL PARADISO

The calle del Paradiso is thus called for « the magnificence with which it used to be adorned and illuminated on the principal solemnities of the church ». The houses along it are characterized by the buttresses supporting the wall on the upper floors so as to allow, with the recessed ground floor a greater width of the street.
They are apartment houses which in some parts display the Gothic origins of their construction.
Gothic, too, is the arch with triangular cusp, with the image of the Madonna placed at its head to correspond with the bridge that leads to the campo Santa Maria Formosa.
These houses belonging to the Foscari family, passed as a dowry to Alvise Mocenigo dalle Zoie on the occasion of his marriage to Pellegrina Foscari in 1491.
The building was begun in 1357 on the initiative of the Abbey of Pomposa, under the Abbot Andrea.

THE VAN AXEL PALACE

THE MARCELLO PINDEMONTE PALACE

224

From the Ponte del Cristo placed at the confluence of three rios, on the right rises the grandiose Marcello-Pindemonte Palace, originally in Gothic style, property of Doge Nicolò Marcello; in the 17th Century, possibly to a plan by Longhena, the façades were re-built. At the end of the fondamenta Sanudo is the entrance to the grandiose and beautiful Soranzo-Van Axel Palace, one of the most interesting examples of Gothic architecture, with two façades looking on the San Canciano and della Panada Canals. One enters from the portal on the fondamenta, which still preserves the original wooden doors furnished with iron door-knockers; from the interior arcaded courtyard the original open stairway of two flights leads to the first floor. The building was erected by the Soranzo from 1473 to 1479 following flamboyant Gothic taste. At No. 5999 can be seen the Gothic Bembo Boldù Palace and successively from the Ponte Widmann, the Widmann-Foscari Palace in 17th Century architecture erected to a plan by Baldassare Longhena. The Widmanns were a rich family of merchants who came originally from Carinthia. The interior rooms are decorated with rich stuccoes of the period.

225

CORTE DEL FONTEGO

CORTE BOTTERA

The corte del Fontego and the corte Bottera are two small but characteristic communicating spaces. They are characterized by small, modest buildings going back to the 14th Century, which, even after continuous transformations retain their original Gothic appearance. In both, one can still feel the spirit of the generations who have lived here in these poor old houses and in the communal space provided by the court.

226

227

AT SAN GIOVANNI GRISOSTOMO

THE CORTE DEL MILION AND THE HOMES OF THE POLO FAMILY

The Church of San Giovanni Grisostomo is a Renaissance work by Codussi, (end of the 15th Century). Behind the church the Campiello of the Milion with remains of Byzantine buildings of the 11th and 12th Century, takes the name of « Milion » from the fact that the Polo family possessed some houses here; to this family belonged Marco, the famous Venetian traveller who got as far as the Court of the Great Mogul (1271-1275) and who, during his imprisonment in Genoa, wrote the celebrated book « The Million » giving the chronicle of this voyages. He had been made prisoner by the Genoese in the famous battle of Curzola in 1298.

In Calle della Testa stands the old Casa Grifalconi, a building of the 15th Century, in ogival style, characterized by the arcaded internal courtyard where the original external stairway still exists. This courtyard and the whole building make up one of the most interesting evidences of Venetian building of the first half of the 15th Century.

229

230

CAMPO SAN BORTOLOMIO

The campo, which has in the middle the monument to Carlo Goldoni, the famous Venetian playwright of the 18th Century, given its position, is midway between the sestieri of San Marco, Cannaregio and San Polo, and thus an obligatory meeting point and passage way.
Among the buildings forming the sides of the campo, the oldest is certainly the Moro Palace, going back to the 14th Century, with the characteristic brick façade in which can be seen even older elements. From this house it is possible to see in the background the central stairway of the Rialto Bridge.

A CITY CENTRE OF GREAT IMPORTANCE FOR STROLLING AND APPOINTMENTS

231

232

THE GRAND CANAL

Beyond all praise

IF WE TRAVEL ALONG THE GRAND CANAL BY DAY OR BY NIGHT, THE CHARM IS PRESENT IN EVERY ELEMENT AND IN EVERY DETAIL OF THE CITY OF WHICH IT IS COMPOSED

233

234

233 The Grand Canal from the Rialto Bridge
234 The Rialto Bridge
235 The Grand Canal at the Rialto
236 « The Rialto Bridge » (J. de Barbari)
237 « The Rialto Bridge », V. Carpaccio
(detail)

235

THE BRIDGE
OF THE RIALTO

AN ANCIENT WOODEN BRIDGE WHICH COULD BE RAISED IN THE MIDDLE.

THE REBUILDING CARRIED OUT IN STONE WITH ONE SINGLE ARCH

From the very earliest times a bridge, first of boats, then of wood on piles, opening in its central portion, united the two banks of the canal. After much pondering, and after having commissioned various projects, the most famous of which was that of Palladio, only in 1588 was it decided to build a stone bridge, to the design of Antonio Da Ponte, who had as his collaborator his nephew Antonio Contin.
In the year 1591 the bridge was completed, even in the upper part which was destined to accommodate a series of shops.

236

FONDAMENTA DEL VIN

FONDAMENTA DEL CARBON

237

THE MANIN PALACE
THE HOME
OF THE LAST DOGE

A building erected by the Dolfin family towards the middle of the 16th Century, to the design of Jacopo Sansovino. The interior was transformed when the building passed into the hands of Ludovico Manin in the 18th Century.

THE BEMBO PALACE
HERE CARDINAL BEMBO
HISTORIOGRAPHER OF THE
REPUBLIC WAS BORN

Palazzo Bembo is a large Gothic building of the 16th Century, very probably erected in successive periods on a primitive Byzantine structure.

238

239

BYZANTINE HOUSES AND PALACES:
THE PALACES OF THE BARZIZZA, BUSINELLO AND DONÀ FAMILIES

A series of Byzantine buildings remains as a witness of the building activity of the 12th and 13th Centuries, along the right bank of the Grand Canal.
They were in part re-built and tampered with, but preserve architectonic elements evident in the ground floor arcades and the many-mullioned windows of the upper floors.

240

THE COCCINA-TIEPOLO PALACE
A splendid dwelling

THE DANDOLO AND LOREDAN PALACES

The two Palaces, divided by a calle both go back to the end of the 12th Century.
The traditional motives of the Byzantine warehouses developed in a truly courtly fashion with arcades on the ground floor and a loggia on the main floor, which here runs the length of the façade.
The two structures have been heightened by two storeys.

Built towards the middle of the 16th Century by Giangiacomo dei Grigi, the building is characterized by two splendid main floors, once famous for the valuable art collections which the various owners arranged in the rooms. The recessed wing, giving on the little garden was built in the second half of the 19th Century.

241

242

THE GRIMANI PALACE
THE MAGNIFICENT FESTIVITIES FOR THE CROWNING OF THE DOGARESSA MOROSINA MOROSINI

Built to the design of Michele Sanmicheli, towards the first half of the 16th Century.
The wish of the proprietor to give to his own dwelling a character of monumentality is evident from the architect's realization, in the grandiose arches of the huge windows, the deep colonnaded atrium on the ground floor, and the strongly projecting stringcourses of the different storeys.

244

THE CAVALLI PALACE

So-called from the two horses in the crest of the coat-of-arms on the façade. The building is of the middle of the 15th Cent. in flamboyant Gothic.

Following the Corner dei Cavalli Palace we see the little Tron palaces, these, too, in the Gothic style of the 15th Century.

243

THE DONÁ PALACE

One of the Donà Palaces, altered in the 16th and 17th Centuries; of the former Byzantine building remains the many-mullioned window.

245

A BUILDING IN THE STYLE OF CODUSSI
THE CORNER-SPINELLI PALACE

Here in the façade one recognizes the architectonic elements of the Vendramin Calergi Palace.
This analogy suggests the name of Mauro Codussi as the architect.
The structure may be dated between the end of the 15th and beginning of the 16th Century. Towards 1542 the interior was in part transformed by Michele Sanmicheli.

246

It is one of the most interesting Gothic buildings in this tract of the Grand Canal; built around 1442 for the family of the same name. There is considerable richness in the architectonic elements of the façade and in the external stairway in the rear courtyard.

THE BERNARDO PALACE

FRANCESCO SFORZA, COUNT OF MILAN, AND BIANCA VISCONTI: GUESTS OF THE SERENISSIMA REPUBLIC

THE GIUSTINIAN GRIMANI PALACE

The present building rose in the early years of the 16th Century in the place of an old Byzantine edifice. The façade, decorated with polychrome marbles is reminiscent of the style of the Lombardo school.

THE MOCENIGO HOMES

The Mocenigo family owned a series of Gothic buildings in this tract of the Grand Canal.
Towards 1580 the building of the first structure, « Casa Nova », was begun. The last, called « Casa Vecchia », was transformed internally and the façade was completely renewed in the 17th Century. These two buildings were later on united by two identical structures that mirrored each other.

In the first Palace Giordano Bruno dwelt in 1592, denounced by his host to the Holy Office; and in 1621 Countess Anne of Shrewsbury, whose relation with the patrician Antonio Foscarini brought this latter a charge of treason against the State, and shortly afterwards his condemnation to death.

THE PISANI-MORETTA PALACE

Gothic style is happily expressed in this building with its huge many-mullioned quadrilobate windows, differing in design between the first and second storeys.
The building dates from the middle of the 15th Century.

THE CONTARINI DALLE FIGURE PALACE
JACOPO CONTARINI PROTECTOR AND FRIEND OF PALLADIO

The name derives from two caryatids which support the balcony.
It is a Renaissance building of the beginning of the 16th Century attributed to Scarpagnino.
The arrangement of the façade derives clearly from the Lombardos.

THE MORO-LIN PALACE
TWO GOTHIC PALACES UNITED BEHIND ONE FAÇADE

It is the result of the structuring and joining of two Gothic buildings originally divided by a narrow « calle », combined in the new building and corresponding to the central fillet of the opening.
The project is attributed to Sebastiano Mazzoni who executed it around 1670 for the painter Pietro Liberi.

This stands « in volta de canal » at the point where the rio of San Pantalon flows into the Grand Canal. It was built between 1582 and 1590, it would appear to the design of Alessandro Vittoria.

THE BALBI PALACE
ON THE BEND OF THE CANAL

253

THE FOSCARI PALACE

THE GIUSTINIAN PALACES

THE SUMPTUOUS HOME OF DOGE FRANCESCO
WAGNER COMPOSED HERE " TRISTAN AND ISOLDE "

The first, at the junction of the
canals was built around 1452 to
become the home of Doge Francesco
Foscari, one of the most important
political figures of the time.
On his death, however, in 1457, the
Palace was still unfinished.
It is one of the most important
buildings on the Grand Canal, with
two very high main floors, the
central rooms of which are
embellished by large, elegant
windows.
Both the Foscari Palace and the
Giustinian Palace are attributed
to Giovanni and Bartolomeo Bon,
very famous architects operating
in the first half of the 15th
Century in the Gothic epoch.
The Giustinian Palaces are two
identical structures mirroring
each other, with the central portal
corresponding to the dividing calle.

254

THE GRASSI PALACE

FAÇADE WITH ONE SIDE ON
CAMPO SAN SAMUELE

256

THE REZZONICO PALACE

255

With its principal façade on the
Grand Canal and the lateral one
on the campo San Samuele where
stands the ancient bell-tower of the
church of the same name going back
to the 12th Cent., the Grassi family
had this sumptuous dwelling built
beginning in 1748, entrusting the
work to Giorgio Massari who
completed it around 1776.

The building of the palace was begun in 1667 by B. Longhena for the Bon family. In 1682 when the artist died, the building had arrived at the first floor.
The work was taken up again with the new owners, the Rezzonicos, in 1750, under the direction of Giorgio Massari who completed the building of the second storey, respecting Longhena's design, and made modifications in the rear portion of the building with the courtyard, the monumental stairway, the splendid ball-room (24 x 14 x 12 metres).

THE **CA' REZZONICO** EIGHTEENTH CENTURY MUSEUM

THE PALACE AND ITS ANCIENT FURNISHINGS

On the ceiling is the magnificent fresco by G. Battista Crosato finished in 1753 (approx.). The subject represents allegories of the four parts of the world.
The furniture in this room, among it the wooden statues of negro slaves and the high-backed arm chairs are the work of Antonio Brustolon, (1700-1723).
The Room of the Wedding Allegory: is so-called from the fresco on the ceiling executed by G. Battista Tiepolo on the occasion of the marriage of Lodovico Rezzonico to Faustina Savorgnan.
By a small stairway one goes down to the mezzanine, the three small rooms of which constituted the apartment of Pope Clement XIII of the family of Rezzonico.
In these rooms the English poet, Robert Browning stayed for a while, and died here in 1889.
The Pastel Room, is so named from the series of portraits in pastel and miniatures by Rosalba Carriera.
The Tapestry Room: on the walls are Flemish tapestries with « Stories of Solomon and the Queen of Sheba ».
The Throne Room: in 1758 G. Battista Tiepolo frescoed the ceiling with an extremely luminous composition representing « The Allegory of Merit ».
The gilded throne was used by Pope Pius VI during a short stay in Venice.
The Tiepolo Room: has a canvas painted by Giambattista between 1744 and 1745.
The Brustolon Room: with an important series of furniture by the Venetian artist.
Going up to the second « main floor » we enter the Portego Room.
The Guardi Room: with three frescoes attributed to Francesco Guardi.
The Alcove Bedroom: where a Venetian bedroom has been reconstructed.
Among the effects is a small coffer for a wedding trousseau, and a toilet service.
The Green Lacquer Room: here are displayed about thirty pieces of drawing room furniture, all lacquered in green and gold with decorations and chinoiserie in accordance with the fashion of those days.
On the walls is a curious painting showing « The frozen lagoon » in the very hard winter of 1788.
The Longhi Room: on the ceiling « The Triumph of Zephyrus and Flora » one of the most significant youthful works of G. Battista

On the walls 34 paintings by Pietro Longhi, interesting and pleasing, more for the subject treated than for their pictorial quality. It is a gallery of scenes, costumes and usages in the private life of Venetians, full of comments expressed in satirical good humour, on everyday life:
« The Morning Chocolate »,
« My Lady's Toilet »,
« Polenta », « The painter's studio »,
« The ride on horseback »,
« The visit to the Convent »,
« The Family Concert »,
« The Domino », « The Furlana »,
« The chemist's shop », « The Moor's Embassy », « The Spice Vendor »,
« The Rhinoceros ».
The Ridotto Room: with the two famous canvases by Guardi « The Ridotto Room » and « The Nuns' Parlour ».
The rich Venetian society used to foregather in the famous Ridotto Rooms (or Gaming Rooms) of San Moisè or in the Nuns' Parlour at San Zaccaria

261

Now one enters a series of small rooms in which have been reconstructed the interior rooms of Tiepolo's villa at Zianigo, frescoed by G. Domenico Tiepolo. The artist, freed from the influence of his father, interprets freely the frivolous world of Venice, underlining the gay character of this apparently trouble-free society during the holiday period in the Veneto countryside along the banks of the River Brenta. « The portego of the New World », dated 1791, where a charlatan demonstrates to a crowd of country folk the novelties and advantages of

262

363

264

a different society; « The minuet in the Villa » where an openair dance is described; and « A Promenade for Three » showing a lady walking with two swains. In another little room the dominating figure is the clown, who is dressed in white and masked, and who under the guise of a buffoon, masks his own symbolism. « The House of the Saltimbancos » (Acrobats); « Clowns at Rest », and «Clown in Love ». The veiled sadness conveyed by this last fresco is entirely absent from the fresco on the ceiling where we see the clowns disporting themselves freely in the scene « The Swing Game ». From here we go up to the third floor where there is a collection of numerous series of objects (porcelain, chinoiserie, ceramics, costumes, etc.). Very interesting is the reconstruction of an old-time chemist's shop, complete with furnishings, jars for herbs, glasses, with the laboratory, a burner, a still, retorts, and phials. The marionette theatre, an amusement dear to Venetians, which was held in the public theatres, in the houses of patricians and even in the squares, has numerous original 18th Century marionettes.

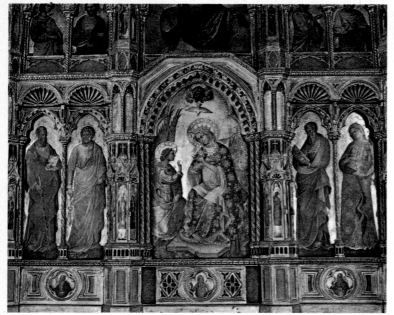

The Gothic church of Santa Maria della Carità and the ex monastery on the courtyard of which one can still see the remaining wing of the cloister erected by Palladio around 1552, are now used as an Institute of Art. Nearby is the edifice of the Scuola della Carità, one of the six Great Scuole of the city. And here is the entrance to the Galleries of the Accademia, which house the most valuable Venetian collection.

THE ACADEMY GALLERIES

265

THE HISTORY OF VENETIAN PAINTING FROM THE FOURTEENTH TO THE EIGHTEENTH CENTURY

Up the great 18th Century stairway we come to the Chapter Room where we can admire the original ceiling, carved and gilded in 1484 by Marco Cozzi of Vicenza.
In this room are displayed numerous altar pieces and panels with gold backgrounds, the work of Venetian masters between the 14th Century and the first half of the 15th Century.

Among the most important works: « Polyptych with figures of Saints and episodes in the Life of Christ and of St. Francis », « Madonna enthroned and child », by Paolo Veneziano.
A great polyptych in two orders by Lorenzo Veneziano representing « The Annunciation and Saints » (1357); « St. James the Greater among four Saints », and « The

Coronation of the Virgin » of the middle of the 15th Century by Michele Giambono.
By Antonio Vivarini « The marriage of St. Monica » and « A Madonna and child ».
Finally two great panels by Jacobello del Fiore, representing « The Coronation of the Virgin » and « Justice between two Archangels ».

266

267

265 Polyptych, Lorenzo Veneziano (detail)
266 Polyptych, Paolo Veneziano (detail)
267 « The Madonna enthroned », Nicolò di Pietro (detail)

PAOLO AND LORENZO VENEZIANO
JACOBELLO DEL FIORE
MICHELE GIAMBONO
ANTONIO VIVARINI
NICOLÒ DI PIETRO

In the second room are collected works by Giovanni Bellini: « The Sacred Conversation » (1480-1490), « The Mourning of Christ »; and by Cima da Conegliano « The Incredulity of St. Thomas » and « The Madonna of the Orange Tree ». Room III: with canvases by painters working between the end of the 15th and the first half of the 16th Cent. (Sebastiano del Piombo, Bernardino Licinio).
Room IV: houses three valuable paintings of the Italian 15th Cent. « St. George » by Andrea Mantegna (1464), « St. Jerome » by Piero della Francesca (mid. 15th Cent.) and « Madonna and Child » by Cosmè Tura.
Room V: dedicated to works by Giovanni Bellini, where the grandeur and originality of the Venetian master is evident, particularly in the « Madonna of the little Trees » (1487), in the « Pietà » and in the lovely Madonnas with Saints. Furthermore, this room has one of the most famous paintings by Giorgione, « The Tempest » (1505-1507) which marks an important moment in the process of innovation in taste and in the conception of composition in Venetian painting.
By the same artist, « Portrait of an Old Woman » expressed in terms that are outstandingly realistic.
Room VI: with painters of the 16th Century among whom are Bonifacio de' Pitati, Jacopo Tintoretto and Paris Bordone.
Room VII: one of Lorenzo Lotto's most fascinating portraits: « Gentleman in his Study ».
Rooms VIII and IX: de' Pitati, J. Palma the E., Romanino, Previtali.
Room X: here are displayed the greatest exponents of Venetian painting of the second half of the 16th Cent., Titian, Jacopo Tintoretto, Paolo Veronese.
The Tintoretto canvases belong to the cycle executed for the main hall of the Scuola San Marco with episodes from the Evangelist's life. The most famous is « The miracle of Saint Mark » (1545-1548).
On the right-hand wall as one enters is the great painting by Veronese, « The Feast in the House of Levi » (1573). The scene is of a pleasant grandiosity and serene wealth, emphasized by splendid open architecture, the costumes of the guests and the many realistic details, all carefully annotated.
In the case of this canvas the painter was compelled to eliminate certain figures considered profane as regards the subject, in the minds of the Court of the Inquisition; the title, which was originally « The Last Supper » also had to be changed.

268 « The marriage of St. Catherine », Lorenzo Veneziano
269 « The Madonna and Child », Cosmè Tura

270

THE SAINT URSULA CYCLE BY CARPACCIO

Room XI: with numerous canvases by Veronese, among them « The Marriage of St. Catherine », a work of his maturity; other works of a historical or mythological character, such as « The Battle of Lepanto », and « The Allegory of Venice ».
In the second part of the room is a group of 17th and 18th Cent. masters, not Venetians, such as Luca Giordano and Francesco Solimena.
Room XII: with Venetian landscape painters of the 18th Cent. among them Giuseppe Zais, Marco Ricci and the Tuscan, Francesco Zuccarelli.

Room XIII: in addition to a series of portraits by Tintoretto, works by Leandro and Jacopo Bassano.
Room XIV: dedicated to painters of the 17th Century; Domenico Fetti, Jan Lys, Bernardo Strozzi.
Room XV: canvases by Giambattista Tiepolo: « The Holy Family », and « San Gaetano ».
Room XVI: here are paintings by Gian Battista Piazzetta, the last great Venetian who concludes the Michelangelesque reform and opens a new current which we see taken up and followed by Tiepolo.
The canvas to be admired is the famous « Fortune Teller » (1740) the young, lively figure of a woman

with a shrewd smile almost of invitation.
Other good portraits by Pietro and Alessandro Longhi.
Room XVII: divided into three sections, the first dedicated to landscape artists, with Canaletto, Francesco Guardi, Michele Marieschi, and Antonio Diziani; the second to figure painters with sketches by Sebastiano Ricci, Gian Battista Piazzetta, Jacopo Amigoni and G. Battista Pittoni; the third section with Tiepolo (sketch for the fresco on the ceiling of the Church of the Scalzi), Pietro Longhi (some of his characteristic genre paintings) and Rosalba Carriera (a group of pastels).
Room XIX: works of the end of the 15th and beginning of the 16th Century (Antonello da Saliba, Pietro da Messina, Vincenzo Catena).
Room XX: here are displayed the great canvases, at one time in the Scuola di S. Giovanni Evangelista, representing the miracles of the relic of the true Cross.
It is a magic moment for Venetian painting and for the city itself which presents a rich, evocative picture in the views which these paintings employ as a background for the episodes narrated.
The city, with its architecture, its people, the nobility, the government, are here before our eyes, re-creating unforgettable moments of art, of history, and of costume: « The miracle of the relic which fell into the Canal of San Lorenzo » (1500) and « The procession in Piazza San Marco » (1496) by Gentile Bellini; « The miraculous healing of a Demoniac at Rialto » by Vittore Carpaccio.
The precision of the various particulars make this painting famous, not only for the history of costume but also for the knowledge of the architectonic appearance of the city before the intervention of transformations carried out in the 16th Century.
The other canvases are by Giovanni Mansueti: « Miracle at St. Lio » and « The miraculous healing at San Polo », in which is seen the interior of a Venetian house of the period;

271

ALVISE VIVARINI

GENTILE BELLINI

VITTORE CARPACCIO

LAZZARO BASTIANI

COSMÈ TURA

ANDREA MANTEGNA

GIOVANNI MANSUETI

by Lazzaro Bastiani « The offering of the relic in the Church of St. John the Evangelist ».
Room XXI: Vittore Carpaccio painted towards the end of the 16th Century the famous canvases for the Scuola di Sant'Orsola, founded in 1306, near the Church of the Saints Giovanni e Paolo. The painter illustrated the significant episodes in the legendary life of the Saint, taken from a chronicle of the 13th Cent. by the writer Jacopo da Varagine. Here one sees clearly the narrative gifts, both pleasant and imaginative of Carpaccio. The scenes, while of foreign cities and places, really develop in Venetian surroundings, minutely described, such as St. Ursula's bedroom; the ceremonies are inspired by the protocol of the Venetian embassies, and the people one sees are the brethren of the Scuola di Sant'Orsola, who were used by the painter as his living models.

272

GIORGIONE
LORENZO LOTTO

273

274

275

270 « The dream of St. Ursula », V. Carpaccio
271 « The Madonna enthroned and Saints », G. Bellini (détail)
272 « The Madonna of the little trees », G. Bellini
273 « The Old Woman », Giorgione
274 « Portrait of a Gentleman », L. Lotto
275 « Portrait of the Procurator Soranzo », J. Tintoretto

Room XXIII situated in the one-time Church of Santa Maria della Carità.
Here are displayed canvases by Bartolomeo Montagna and by Giovanni and Gentile Bellini, Alvise Vivarini and Cima da Conegliano. Room XXIV formerly the Albergo della Scuola with the richly carved ceiling dating back to 1496. Two important works are « The Presentation of the Virgin at the Temple » by Titian (1538) and the triptych « The Virgin and Child enthroned among the Doctors of the Church » by Antonio Vivarini and Giovanni Alemagna, of considerable decorative effect due to the polychrome painting of the figures and the gold background.

TITIAN
VERONESE
TINTORETTO

276

277

278

276 « The Presentation in the Temple », Ti■
277 « The Last Supper », P. Veronese
278 « The freeing of the slave », J. Tintoret■
279 « The fortune teller », G.B. Piazzetta
280 « Landscape with a bull hunt », F. Zucca■
281 « David », D. Fetti (detail)
282 « St. Mark's Basin », F. Guardi

G.B. PIAZZETTA
G.B. TIEPOLO

THE BASSANO
FRANCESCO ZUCCARELLI ·
GIUSEPPE ZAIS
CANALETTO
FRANCESCO GUARDI
PIETRO AND ALESSANDRO
LONGHI

THE LOREDAN PALACE

Termed the Ambassador's because in the 18th Century it was the seat of the Roman Ambassadors. The construction is 15th Century Gothic with the typical many-mullioned quadrilobate windows.

THE CONTARINI DAGLI SCRIGNI PALACE

The first, 16th Century Gothic, was transformed internally in the 18th Century by Francesco Smeraldi; the second was designed towards 1610 by Vincenzo Scamozzi as an enlargement of the first.

283

284

THE FRANCHETTI PALACE
A GOTHIC BUILDING OF THE 15th CENTURY PARTLY ALTERED

285

THE BARBARO PALACES
IT WAS THE PALACE OF THE FRENCH AMBASSADOR IN 1499. ISABELLA D'ESTE LIVED HERE FOR SOME TIME.

These two adjacent houses, the first Gothic of the 14th-15th Century, the second of the 17th Century, were probably the result of a transformation of a previously existing house.

THE CONTARINI DAL ZAFFO PALACE
A RENAISSANCE FAÇADE

Built towards the end of the 15th Century and terminated in the very early years of the 16th Century. There is some doubt whether Codussi or Lombardo was the designer of this.

286

THE CASINA DELLE ROSE
THE VENETIAN RESIDENCE OF D'ANNUNZIO AND CANOVA

287

289

THE CORNER DELLA CA' GRANDE PALACE

The building was commissioned by Jacopo Cornaro between 1532 and 1561 to a design by Jacopo Sansovino. The façade is contained within the geometrical figure of a square, subdivided into three horizontal strips by the string courses and the strongly projecting balconies. The square courtyard at the rear is included in the body of the structure.

THE BIONDETTI PALACE
ROSALBA CARRIERA LIVED AND DIED HERE

A modest little house tucked in between the Venier and Centani Palace (18th Century) and the Da Mula Gothic style Palace.

291

THE GRITTI PALACE
A MODERN HOTEL IN A GOTHIC BUILDING

At one time the façade of the building was frescoed by Giorgione; now one sees the bare brickwork.

AN UNFINISHED PALACE
THE VENIER DEI LEONI PALACE

The intention of the patrons and of the architect Lorenzo Boschetti, who planned it around 1749 was to build an edifice of enormous proportions, but the idea was interrupted at ground floor level for lack of funds due to the changed fortunes of the patrons.

THE DARIO PALACE

Built around 1487 for Giovanni Dario, Secretary of the Republic in Constantinople, to the design of Pietro Lombardo.
The façade is characteristic, not only for its oblique angle due to the subsidence of the foundations, but also for the great attention to detail and for the decorations and inlays of polychrome marbles.

292

THE FLANGINI-FINI PALACE

Of the end of the 17th Century, attributed to Alessandro Tremigon.

THE MANOLESSO PALACE

Originally Gothic, it was later heightened and amplified.

THE CONTARINI PALACE
THE LEGENDARY HOME OF DESDEMONA

A small building, rich in architectonic and decorative elements in flamboyant Gothic style (1475 ca). The design of the balcony on the first main floor is interesting.

THE TERRIBLE PLAGUE IN 1630 HAD DECIMATED THE POPULATION OF VENICE AND WEAKENED THEIR RESISTANCE AND WILL-POWER

294

SANTA MARIA DELLA SALUTE

THE BUILDING OF THE VOTIVE TEMPLE WAS A PUBLIC REACTION TO THE SCOURGE

295

THE CENTRAL PLAN USED BY LONGHENA IN THE SALUTE WAS AN ABSOLUTE NOVELTY FOR VENICE AND REPRESENTS A BREAK WITH THE PERSISTENT PALLADIAN TRADITION.

296

THE COLLECTIONS IN THE SEMINARY

294 Santa Maria della Salute, the façade
295 Santa Maria della Salute Church
296 The Salute, detail of the buttresses
297 The Salute, the dome
298 The church of the Salute and the Seminary.

98

The temple was built by Longhena between 1631 and 1681.
The interior is on a central plan, octagonal with an ambulatory from which open six chapels and, on the axis of the main entrance, the presbytery.
The composite pilasters support the drum on which rises the great dome, while a second, smaller dome, flanked by two small belltowers, is placed so as to cover the presbytery.
The Church is built on a raised platform to allow the development of a wide flight of steps which serves to emphasize the celebrational function of the edifice.
Above the altar is the image of the Virgin, a picture of the Greek-Byzantine school, brought to Venice in 1672 from the Isle of Candia by Francesco Morosini.
In the main Sacristy is the painting by Titian executed around 1512 and representing « St. Mark among the Saints ».
Next to the Church is the Patriarchal Seminary which houses a museum and a Picture Gallery.

297

298

299

THE PUNTA DELLA DOGANA DA MAR
DIVIDES THE ENTRANCE OF THE GRAND CANAL FROM THE GIUDECCA CANAL

300

Dogana da Mar (The Customs House) was built towards the year 1677 by the architect Giovanni Benoni. The part towards the point is in the form of a tower surmounted by a gilded sphere symbolizing Fortune. Here till the 16th Century goods were unloaded and tolls paid.

301

302

303

BEYOND THE CANAL OF THE **GIUDECCA ISLAND,** **THE SPINALUNGA** FOR THE OLD VENETIANS

304

The name Giudecca derives from the fact that probably in earlier times the island was inhabited almost entirely by Jews.

It closes the city off on the south from the lagoon proper, forming the wide canal of the same name.

At one time its depth was very considerably less than it is to-day and more or less approximated that of the modern series of longitudinal canals.

Successive fillings-in have permitted new areas of ground to be obtained. Building activity, however, has developed only in this century; in addition to housing settlements numerous factories have sprung up, many to-day have nevertheless been abandoned, among which stands out, for its bulk and for its architectonic characterization, the Stucky-Mill.

Along the water-front are remains of the Renaissance Visconti House, the Church of Sant'Eufemia, the Vendramin Palace, of the Doge Andrea, rebuilt to the design of J. Sansovino.

ALONG THE OUTLINE OF THE HOUSES AND PALACES
THE HOSPICE OF THE ZITELLE EMERGES AND
THE CHURCH OF THE REDENTORE

305

At one time there were also numerous convents on the island (now almost all disappeared) and Churches, among which the Church of the Redeemer built to the design of Andrea Palladio between 1577 and 1592, the year of its consecration. This church was erected after the end of the 1576 Plague.

The hospice of the Zitelle was also erected by Palladio and constituted a model for all the hospices that were built in Venice in the following centuries, with the church in the centre tucked in between the two structures of the hospice.

306

307

308

A STROLL ALONG THE EMBANKMENT **OF THE ZATTERE** IN SPRING AND AUTUMN

So called because it was here the rafts carrying timber berthed. The long water-front which runs along the entire southern margin of the city from Punta della Dogana to San Basilio, faces the Giudecca Canal, named after the island facing it.

309

THE HOSPICE OF THE INCURABILI

On the Zattere bank, much frequented by Venetians in the intermediate seasons as a pleasant walk because of its excellent southern exposure, rises the Hospital degli Incurabili founded in 1522 and later transformed into a hospice for young orphans. It became famous for its musical oratory.
Jacopo Sansovino had erected the Church (unfortunately demolished in 1821) which served as an auditorium for concerts.

310

311

312

313

Go along the characteristic waters-fronts and pass through silent little squares that connect internally the areas of the Salute and the Accademia.

This is an extremely evocative part of the city, characterized by an old-time building system, the result of successive changes in the 15th and up to the 18th Century. Little palaces, more modest rented houses, rows of working-class type dwellings; no great palace, because these all face the Grand Canal, and only the backs and the entrance courtyards are to be seen on this side.

FROM THE ACCADEMIA TO THE SALUTE

314

315

316

317

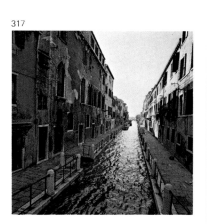

308 Le Zattere
309 Hospice degli Incurabili (chronic invalids)
310, 311 The Incurabili, Heads on the side doorways
312 Fondamenta delle Zattere
313 Rio terrà dei Catecumeni (proselytes)
314 The church and Scuola del Santo Spirito
315 Rio di San Vio
316 Rio delle Torreselle
317 Rio della Fornace

318

THE GESUATI

The company of the poor Gesuati built an oratory here dedicated to St. Jerome, between 1494 and 1524. Its Renaissance façade can still be seen to-day.
The order was suppressed because the brethren went beyond the terms of their ministry, and at that point the Dominicans took over, and it was they who built the Church, still called « dei Gesuati ».
It was begun in 1726 to a plan by Giorgio Massari, and ended in the year 1736.
On the ceiling, among decorations and stuccoes are three luminous frescoes by Gian Battista Tiepolo (1737-39); in the side chapels altar pieces by the same Tiepolo, Piazzetta and Tintoretto.

TIEPOLO PAINTED THE CEILING OF THE CHURCH

320

319

321

CAMPO SAN BASEGIO
AND THE CALLE DEL VENTO

A HOUSE FOR RENTED FLATS

The short calle del Vento whose name obviously derives from the strong currents of air which come from the Giudecca Canal, leads from the square of San Basegio to the bank of the Zattere. The house standing isolated to the right of the junction of the canals is a typical 16th Century apartment house, built with speculative intent and thus furnished with numerous apartments which the proprietor let.

SAN TROVASO

A CHURCH WITH TWO FAÇADES AND AN ANCIENT BOAT-BUILDING YARD

The Church of San Trovaso, founded in the 9th Century and re-built many times in the following centuries, assumed its aspect early in the 17th Century to the design of Francesco Smeraldi, follower and continuer in Venice of Palladian models.
The works began in the year 1585. There are two façades, one facing the actual square and the other looking on the canal of the same name with the low, robust belltower beside it. Inside are paintings by Tintoretto, Michele Giambono, J. Palma the Y.
The raised campo with the well at its centre served to accommodate the chests of clay for the purification of the rain water which was then put into the well and drinkable.

THE NANI PALACE

At the junction of the two canals one of the last surviving boat-yards of Venice, where gondolas and boats used to be built or repaired. Along the rio of San Trovaso in the Brandolin-Sangiantoffetti Palace of mid-16th Century; the Nani Palace, once the property of the Barbarigo family, in Gothic 15th Century style.

322 The church of San Trovaso, façade
323 The area round San Trovaso
324 The San Trovaso gondola building yard
325 The Nani Palace

CAMPO SANTA MARGHERITA: A GAY OPEN SPACE

FROM THE TRUNCATED CAMPANILE OF SANTA MARGHERITA TO THE CONVENTUAL GROUP AND THE SCUOLA DEI CARMINI

327

Campo Santa Margherita is one of the oldest centres of the life of the people, animated even to-day in the morning by the fish and vegetable markets.
Here are many Byzantine single-storeyed houses, which were transformed to a certain extent in the Gothic period.
The foundation of the first Church of the Carmini goes back to the 12th Century.
In 1286 the church was re-built and in 1348 consecrated.
The structure is on a basilical plan with three naves with tall columns and 14th Century capitals.
The Gothic structure of the Church was modified at the beginning of the 16th Century in both the apsidal part and the curvilinear-crowned façade.
Between the end of the 16th and beginning of the 17th Century the upper part of the central nave was decorated with wood panelling enriched by sculptures of complete figures and by paintings.
On the right-hand wall above the second altar is an important work by Cima da Conegliano representing « The crib with the Saints Helena and Catherine, the Guardian Angel and Tobias » (approx. 1509).
The dome is decorated with frescoes by Sebastiano Ricci (1708).
In the last span of the central nave are the two wall choirs of the 16th Century with the place for the organ and musicians.
Near the left-hand side door is a valuable painting by Lorenzo Lotto « St. Nicholas, St. Lucy, the Baptist and St. George killing the dragon » (approx. 1530).
The present bell-tower of the beginning of the 17th Century which after a few years began to lean due to the subsidence of the foundations, was straightened and strengthened in 1688 by Giuseppe Sardi.

Next to the Church stands the Scuola dei Carmini, built in the second half of the 17th Century and completed between 1668 and 1670 with the two façades to a design by Longhena. In the 18th Century the decorations of the interior rooms was carried out, concluded in 1744 by Tiepolo.
The great stairway which leads to the upper floor has vaults richly decorated with stuccoes and frescoes.
The ceiling of the upper hall is sub-divided into 9 compartments within which are to be seen the magnificent canvases by Tiepolo, among which, in the centre, « The Virgin in glory hands the scapular to the blessed Simeon Stock ». In the hall of the hostel is an important painting by G. Battista Piazzetta, « Judith and Holofernes ».

328

326 Campo Santa Margherita
327 The Campo and church of the Carmini
328 « The Nativity », in the Carmini, Cima da Conegliano (detail)
329 The campanile of San Barnaba
330 Rio San Barnaba
331 The church of San Barnaba
332 The Ariani Palace

329

330

In the Campo San Barnaba stands the church of the same name, re-built by Lorenzo Boschetti from 1749 to 1776. Of the old church only the characteristic bell-tower remains, going back to the 12th Century, one of the finest in Venice, with the characteristic « pine cone » conical cusp.

On the ponte dei Pugni two factions of the city used to battle with each other, the Castellani (inhabitants of S. Pietro di Castello and the Nicolotti (of S. Nicolò dei Mendicoli). The bridge had no parapet and the contestants tried to push their adversaries into the rio by dint of punches and pushes.

The custom was suppressed at the beginning of the 18th Century because of the many accidents.

331

THE SPLENDID ROW OF WINDOWS OF THE ARIANI PALACE

A building of the second half of the 14th Century.
Above the arches of the many-mullioned window of the second storey is a fine tracery, the design of which constitutes almost a model of an architectonic current developed later in many Venetian palaces.

THE ZENOBIO PALACE

The fondamenta del Soccorso takes its name from the Church and annexed Hospice (at No. 2591), founded towards the 16th Century as an asylum for fallen women by the celebrated poetess and courtesan Veronica Franco.
At No. 2597 the Zenobio Palace, built between 1690 and 1700 by Antonio Gaspari.

THE CHURCH OF SAN PANTALON

The Church of San Pantalon was built between 1668 and 1686; the interior, a single nave has a vaulted ceiling on which Gian Antonio Fumiani painted a single great composition: « The episodes of the martyrdom of S. Pantalon ».

332

SAN SEBASTIANO
THE CHURCH OF THE ANGELO RAFFAELE
SAN NICOLÒ DEI MENDICOLI

333

THREE DIFFERENT PERIODS, THREE EXPRESSIVE MOMENTS IN A SIMPLE WORKING-CLASS QUARTER.

PAOLO VERONESE IN THE CHURCH OF SAN SEBASTIANO

The building with a single nave was erected between 1505 and 1548 by Antonio Abbondi known as Scarpagnino.
The main interest is constituted in the interior by the pictorial cycle by Paolo Veronese.
To follow the work of the painter in this church chronologically the visit begins from the Sacristy; on the ceiling one can admire « The Virgin Crowned and the Evangelists », of 1555.
Returning to the church, in the three central panels of the ceiling Veronese executed « Stories of Queen Esther », 1556.
Shortly afterwards he frescoed the dome of the presbytery, a work unfortunately lost.
Contemporaneously Veronese was preparing the sketches of the frescoes on the walls, which he executed later with the help of his brother Benedetto and others.
The upper frieze is constituted by the architectonic motives of the twisted columns, among which alternate Prophets and Sibyls.
On the arch of the main altar, « The Annunciation » and on the pendentives of the six lateral chapels « The figures of the Apostles ».
Starting in 1559, Veronese executed the altar piece of the main altar with « The Virgin and Child in Glory ».
In the same period he prepared the designs of the organ. On the outside of its doors is represented « The presentation of Jesus at the Temple » and on the inside « The Poor of Bethesda ». On the parapet we see « The Nativity ».
In 1565 he began a new period of work to complete the decoration of the main chapel.
Two great paintings with « Episodes from the life of St. Sebastian ».
The great painter is buried here.

THE CHURCH OF THE ANGELO RAFFAELE
THE STORY OF TOBIAS BY G. ANTONIO GUARDI

The present building goes back to the beginning of the 17th Century and is the work of Francesco Contin. The façade is later, 1735.
The interior, in the form of a Greek cross, houses on the entrance wall the organ on the parapet of which, divided into five compartments, are painted « Stories of Tobias » attributed by some critics to Francesco Guardi, by others to his brother Giovan Antonio.
Behind the church is the campo del Cimitero whose name derives from the existence of the parish cemetery, which in olden days every church had.

334

335

333 The church of San Sebastiano
334 Detail of the frescoes by P. Veronese (S. Sebastiano)
335 The Church of the Angelo Raffaele
336 Rio dell'Angelo Raffaele
337 The church of San Nicolò dei Mendicoli
338 Rio San Nicolò

SAN NICOLÒ DEI MENDICOLI
ONE OF THE OLDEST CHURCHES IN VENICE

It seems that the first building goes back to the 7th Century; in the second half of the 12th Century it was completely re-built together with the nearby isolated bell-tower.

In the 14th Century the Church underwent considerable re-building, among other things the substitution of the capitals in the nave and the roof.

Towards 1580 the interior walls of the central nave were furnished with wooden panelling with ornamental motives, statues alternating with paintings illustrating « Episodes in the Life of Christ ».

Between 1750 and 1760 the little façade towards the square was erected.

The little arcade of the main façade served as a shelter for the Pinzochere or poor women.

SANTA MARIA GLORIOSA DEI FRARI

A FRANCISCAN CHURCH

Even if the building extended over a very long period, the church possesses a sufficiently unitary character, and with the Church of the SS. Giovanni e Paolo, represents one of the most complete and mature expressions of Venetian Gothic.

An early building, begun in the year 1250, was only just finished when the wealth of the Order of the Friars Minor of St. Francis having increased, it was decided to build a new and much larger edifice.

The works began in 1340 at the part of the apses, then continuing with the naves towards the canal. The consecration took place in 1469. The plan is that of an Egyptian cross, in three naves with seven apsidal chapels opening on the transept.

The bell-tower, the work of Jacopo Celega and his sons Pietro and Paolo was finished in 1369.

The planimetric design of the left part of the church is enriched by two chapels added later, the Corner Chapel in 1417 and the Emiliani Chapel in 1432.

339

341

340

On the right side of the church is the monastery with its two cloisters; the monastery buildings now house the State Archives with the valuable collection of the documents of the Republic of Venice, brought here and put together after 1797.

In the space between the last four columns of the central nave towards the transept, according to the liturgical tradition of the time is the large, rich choir of the Friars with priceless wooden stalls in three orders, work of Marco Cozzi (1468) contained within a marble surround with Renaissance reliefs. This is the only choir of its type still existing in Venice, out of the many once to be seen in Gothic churches but destroyed between the 16th and 17th Century. Along the two walls are important funeral monuments which mark the passage from Gothic to Renaissance style.

In the sacristy, added to the fabric in the second half of the 15th Century is the priceless painting depicting « The Virgin and Child with Cherub musicians and Saints » by Giovanni Bellini, dated 1488.

341

343

DONATELLO AND TITIAN

A WOODEN STATUE AND AN ALTARPIECE

In the first apsidal chapel, that of the Bernardo family, is to be seen the polyptych by Bartolomeo Vivarini, signed and dated 1482, representing « Madonna and Child with saints ».

In the third chapel, of the Fiorentini, the important sculpture in painted wood, representing « St. John the Baptist » a marvellous example of the art of Donatello. The central chapel houses Titian's masterpiece, « The Assumption » of 1518, (the Virgin rises up into the heavens among a host of cherubs, while on high stands out the figure of the Eternal Father). There are two very interesting funeral monuments, the first dedicated to the doge Francesco Foscari (second half of 15th Century) attributed to Bartolomeo Bon, the second dedicated to the Doge Nicolò

Tron (died 1473), the sculptural part directed and executed by Antonio Rizzo.

In the third chapel, of the Milanesi, is buried the Chapel Master of San Marco, Claudio Monteverdi, the famous Venetian musician. On the altar, on high « Coronation of the Virgin » by Alvise Vivarini left uncompleted at the death of the painter (1503-1505) and terminated by Marco Basaiti. Next is the funeral monument of Jacopo Pesaro, Bishop of Cyprus, who commissioned Titian to execute the famous painting « The Madonna of Casa Pesaro » placed upon the altar (1526). B. Longhena, as a frame for the lateral door, towards 1669 constructed the grandiose monument to the Doge Giovanni Pesaro who had died ten years earlier.

The composition is of purely Baroque ispiration in the wealth and over-abundance of the architectonic and plastic decoration in high relief; the motive of the caryatids is typical of the artist who had made use of them in other works as well.

THE SCUOLA GRANDE DI SAN ROCCO: A CHARITY
BROTHERHOOD

The building, begun in 1515 went on for fifty years.
Bartolomeo Bon who superintended the works up to the first order was succeeded by Scarpagnino and Giangiacomo dei Grigi who completed the work.
The double mullions on the ground floor are clearly inspired by Codussi.
Scarpagnino planned the addition to the earlier project of the great strongly projecting columns.
Next to the school is the Church of San Rocco, built for a first time at the end of the 15th Century by Bartolomeo Bon, it was later re-built by Giovanni Scalfarotto in 1725; Bernardino Maccaruzzi carried out the work on the new façade between 1765 and 1771.

344

345

346
347

A GALLERY OF MASTERPIECES BY JACOPO TINTORETTO

For this school Tintoretto executed one of the most important cycles of his pictorial activity between 1564 and 1588. In these works the painter who, in these years had arrived at his maturity, expresses completely his artistic conception, wherein the light brings out the movement and dynamic qualities in the composition of the figures expressed in perspective.
In the ground floor hall, along the walls are eight canvases with scenes from the New Testament, among them « The Flight into Egypt » where the landscape plays a leading role.
One arrives at the first floor by means of the monumental stairway with frescoed vault by Pellegrini. In the main hall are 23 canvases, of which Tintoretto finished the ceiling ones by 1578 and those on the walls by 1581.
The subjects of the ceiling canvases, framed within rich decorations, deal with Episodes from the Old Testament (« Moses draws water from the rock », « Moses and the brazen serpent », « The fall of Manna »), while those on the walls are Episodes from the New Testament (« The Birth of Jesus », « The Baptism of Jesus », « Miracles », « The Temptations » « The Last Supper »).
The Hall of the Hostel was originally to have been painted by Titian, but later a competition was announced in which took part Veronese, Salviati, Zuccari and Tintoretto who won it by submitting not just a sketch as had done the other competitors, but with a painting already completed.
The work was carried out rapidly by Tintoretto and in 1566 might be considered finished.
The ceiling, divided into compartments has in the centre « St. Rock in Glory » and in the other panels allegorical representations of the Great Scuole of Venice.
On the walls, « The Crucifixion » signed and dated 1565.
The two canvases representing « Christ bearing the Cross » and « The Dead Christ » are by Titian.

344 The Scuola di San Rocco
345 Campiello di Castelforte
346 « The deposition », J. Tintoretto (Scuola di San Rocco)
347 « The ascent to Calvary », J. Tintoretto (Scuola di S. Rocco)

CAMPO SAN GIACOMO DELL'ORIO
IN THE SESTIERE OF SANTA CROCE

This is one of the main squares in the sestiere di Santa Croce, both for size and for urbanistic characterization, in the middle of a thickly-populated area, through which pass various direct ways from the Railway, from the Frari, from San Polo, from Rialto, towards the built-up strip along the Grand Canal. The Church of very ancient origin and foundation, maintains its original Gothic structure internally with the lovely wooden ceiling very similar to that of the Church of Santo Stefano. Successive modifications, especially of the 16th Century, have changed some parts of the building, in particular, the apses.

The bell-tower which stands isolated at the side of the church is lovely. The building which stands in Campo San Giacomo dell'Orio, looking on to the rio of the same name, was built in 1671 with the express purpose of being an Anatomical Theatre. The custom of dissecting corpses for purposes of study, goes back in Venice to some centuries earlier.

348 The area round San Giacomo dell'Orio
349 The belfry
350 The campo and the church of San Giacomo dell'Orio
351 San Giacomo dell'Orio, the façade of the transept

352

THE TOLENTINI
SANTA MARIA MATER DOMINI
CAMPO SANT'AGOSTINO
CAMPO SAN BOLDO

The Tolentini, (now University Institute of Architecture): this was the name given to the old convent of the Theatine friars dedicated to San Nicolò da Tolentino. The church and the monastery were built between 1591 and 1602 to the design of the architect Vincenzo Scamozzi. The façade was erected much later by Andrea Tirali between the first and second decades of the 18th Century.

Campo Santa Maria Mater Domini is characterized not only by the Codussian church and by Gothic and classic Palaces, but also by Byzantine houses that make up one side of the square with their brickwork façades and 13th Century double mullion windows. Along the canal, too, stand various old buildings going back to the 14th Century, which bear witness to the ancient origin of this area of the city so close to the district of Rialto.

353

354

Until the 19th Century the churches dedicated to St. Boldo and St. Augustine existed in the squares of the same names. Both of very old foundation, going back to the Veneto Byzantine period, they were completely demolished.
At San Boldo there is still the trunk of the brickwork bell-tower.
In Campo Sant'Agostino used to stand the houses of the Tiepolo family to whom belonged the famous Bajamonte who in 1310 headed a plot against the Government of the Republic. When the intrigue was discovered, Bajamonte managed to escape but the Signoria ordered the demolition of the houses and the erection in that place of a « Column of Infamy ». On the opposite side of the rio· the Donà dalle Rose Palace of the early 16th Century; the Molin Palace whose façade was rebuilt in 1806 to match; the Giustinian Palace of the 18th Century; finally the Collalto-Zane Palace to a design by Longhena. The printing house of the famous Aldo Manuzio, Senior, producer of so many beautiful editions of Italian classics in the late 15th Century seems to have existed in Rio Terrà Secondo.

355

356

358

357

359

361

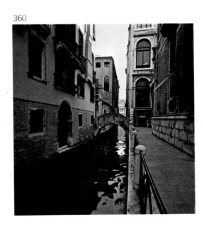

360

THE CHARMING RIO DI **PONTE DELLE TETTE**

ON THE FONDAMENTA DI CA' PESARO

CAMPIELLO ALBRIZZI DOMINATED BY THE SUMPTUOUS SEVENTEENTH CENTURY PALACE

Agnus Dei Palace rises on the opposite part of the canal; it has traces of the old building of the 11th Century in the interior courtyard; the very ornate window on the first floor belongs to the Gothic rebuilding of the 14th Century.

The denomination of the bridge and the fondamenta delle Tette is linked to the presence in these parts of prostitutes who used to stand at windows and doors with their breasts uncovered so as better to attract passers-by. Tradition then in fact makes this custom go back to a law of the government which emanated with the aim of distracting « with such an incentive the idea of men to sin against nature » (Tassini).

The campiello Albrizzi takes its name from the grandiose palace the Albrizzi family had built towards the middle of the 17th Century. Even if the architectonic appearance of the building is purely Baroque in style and proportions, the decoration of the rooms of the interior is of the 18th Century.

359 Ponte delle Tette
360 Fondamenta Pesaro
361 Campiello Albrizzi

CAMPO SAN POLO

ONE OF THE LARGEST OPEN SPACES IN VENICE. HERE THE WEEKLY MARKET, FAIRS, POPULAR FESTIVALS, THEATRICAL PERFORMANCES, BULL AND BEAR FIGHTING ALL TOOK PLACE

Along the sides of the campo stand numerous important buildings.
At the corner along the way towards Rialto stands an elegant Renaissance house of the 15th Century.
Next comes the Tiepolo Palace of the 18th Century attributed to Massari.
The two Soranzo Palaces; the first in flamboyant Gothic style with elegant mullioned windows on the main floor, the second also Gothic but in a style still of the 14th Century.
In the church of San Polo, a building many times altered but with abundant traces both outside and in of its antique Gothic structure, one can admire the little canvases

THE HOME OF BIANCA CAPPELLO

362

363

representing the fourteen stations of the Way of the Cross, painted with pictorial freshness and immediacy in 1749 by Gian Domenico Tiepolo. From an inscription to be seen at the base of the bell-tower, one reads that the elegant structure was erected in 1362.
From the other side of the square, looking on rio di San Polo is the grand Corner-Mocenigo Palace, work of the architect Michele Sanmicheli, known above all in Venice as a specialist in fortifications of a military type.

364

362 The house of Bianca Cappello
363 Campo San Polo
364 Rio San Polo

THE SALVIATI, FLORENTINE BANKERS IN VENICE

The rich Florentine bankers of the Salviati family had one of their centres of business in Venice; the houses of their employees and their business offices were concentrated in buildings along the arcaded water-front that took its name from them.

Not far beyond the ponte Storto on the other side of the canal is the Cappello Palace. Here lived the young and beautiful Bianca Cappello, and from here she fled to Florence in 1563 with Pietro Bonaventuri, a Florentine employee of the nearby Salviati Bank. Introduced then into the court of the Medici, she became the mistress and then the wife of the Grand Duke of Tuscany, Francesco de' Medici. She died not long afterwards, in mysterious circumstances, possibly poisoned.

365

THE CENTANI PALACE
THE BIRTH-PLACE OF THE GREAT VENETIAN PLAYWRIGHT CARLO GOLDONI

The Centani-Rizzi Palace whose Gothic façade looks on the canal of San Tomà, following its strongly curved line. Its principal entrance is from the calle which opens into a characteristic Gothic courtyard with an open stairway leaning against the boundary wall. Here, in 1707 was born the most famous Venetian playwright, Carlo Goldoni. From his first theatrical compositions, still traditional as regards plot and devolopment, the author developed 'a new kind of theatre, more realistic and linked also to the subjects and customs of his time, from which he draws a complete, somewhat critical and ironic picture in the many plays he wrote and presented in the principal theatres of Venice; comedies which made him justly famous and where his genius as a playwright is expressed in a new and reformatory form and content. Now the building is the seat of an Institute of theatrical studies with a rich library dealing with the life and works of Goldoni and the 18th Century Venetian theatre in general.

367

365 Sottoportico Salviati
366 The Centani Palace, courtyard
367 Portrait of Carlo Goldoni

THE RIALTO MARKET, COMMERCIAL CENTRE OF THE CITY

From the very foundation of the city, in addition to the political religious centre of St. Mark's Square, at the same time the economic centre of the Rialto area was developing.

Little by little vast areas of sand-banks and pools were drained, and suitable buildings were erected to house the goods which were exchanged on the Rialto square, together with offices for the merchants and agents and for the allied administration.

Each in his special area, were to be found the fish market, the Fruit and Vegetable markets, the workshops of the goldsmiths, of those who sold materials, spices and raw materials in general.

On the fondamenta del Carbon and that del Vin, boats and ships of every kind used to be moored, loaded with merchandise, and there was an incessant bustle of exchanges.

The houses which nowadays go from the Ruga degli Orefici to the Church of San Silvestro often used to be the property of the various communities (Germans, Tuscans etc.) present with goods from their own parts to sell or exchange in the market.

Among the first buildings in the high area were the Beccheria (Butcher's Shop) and the Pescheria (Fish-market).

COURTS OF JUSTICE, DEPOTS WAREHOUSES, SHOPS, EXCHANGE BANKS

THE CHURCHES OF SAN GIACOMETTO AND SAN GIOVANNI ELEMOSINARIO

Contemporaneously rose the Church of San Giovanni Elemosinario, many times re-built, its final rebuilding going back to the period between 1527 and 1539, to a model by Scarpagnino, and the Church of San Giacomo di Rialto, on the square of the same name, which even to-day maintains internally the 12th Century structure.

THE PALACE OF THE CAMERLENGHI

THE PALACE OF THE TEN SAVI

THE FABBRICHE VECCHIE

THE FABBRICHE NUOVE

The Dieci Savi Palace, the minor façade of which looks on to the Grand Canal, goes back internally for a long way, as far as the Ruga Vecchia of San Giovanni Elemosinario.

It was built following the great fire of 1514, between 1520 and 1522 to the plan of Antonio Scarpagnino. The building of the Fabbriche Nuove (New Buildings) of Rialto, attributed to Sansovino, was carried out between 1552 and 1555.

NARANZERIA

RUGA DEGLI OREFICI

PORTICO OF BANCO GIRO

ERBARIA

CAMPO DELLA PESCARIA

PANETTERIA

CAMPO DELLE BECCARIE

RIVA DELL'OLIO

CASARIA

RIVA DEL VIN

RIVA DEL CARBON

370

THE GRAND CANAL FROM THE RIALTO TO SANTA LUCIA

THE FIRE IN 1514

371

There was a constant bustle of activity and the market was more prosperous than ever when in 1514 a terrible fire broke out, which spread rapidly to the entire area, destroying immense and incalculable wealth of both buildings and goods.
The Republic intervened with considerable solicitude, saving, with the help of soldiers, what it was possible to save and starting the work of rebuilding without delay, since the good of the entire city depended on the normal functioning of the market and business.
Following the scheme of the preceding ones, the long high houses in series were built, separated by long, narrow calle which we see to-day, the ground floor used as a warehouse or shops and the upper as offices or dwellings.
The Church of San Giovanni was rebuilt as were the Fabbriche Vecchie (Old Buildings) to the plan of Scarpagnino, characterized by arcades all along the front elevation; at the same time the characteristic Campo di San Giacometto was reconstituted.
In this campo the rich Venetian nobles, either through their agents, or personally, opened pawn-shops carrying on side by side with the real market, a considerable volume of financial activity.
Here galleys headed for the East were hired out on contract.
In the campo stands the famous column, supported by a caryatid, known by the Venetians as « Il Gobbo » (the hunchback) from which were proclaimed new laws and Court sentences.
An interesting walk is along the Ruga di San Giovanni Elemosinario which brings one quickly into the campo San Polo.
The calle dei Botteri was so named from the presence of the barrel-makers who had their shops and workshops here.

THE RENAISSANCE PALACE OF THE CAMERLENGHI

THE FONTEGO DEI TEDESCHI
THE GIORGIONE FRESCOES NOW LOST

This building, too, like that of the Turkish Merchants had been let to a foreign community, the Germans.
The building, on a square plan with an arcaded interior courtyard was re-built following a fire and finished around 1508 by Giorgio Spavento and Scarpagnino.
The façade was decorated by frescoes by Giorgione.

The seat of an important Venetian magistracy concerned with the finances of the State and of other lesser magistracies who had on the ground floor the prisons reserved for debtors.
On the site of a one-time loggia of the merchants, the present building was erected between 1525 and 1528, possibly to the design of Guglielmo dei Grigi.

372

368 Rialto marketplace
369 The area round the Rialto

THE CORNER DELLA REGINA PALACE

In 1724 Domenico Rossi began the building, on the site of an earlier palace of the Cornaro family, of the branch known as « the Queen's », descendants of Caterina Cornaro, queen of Cyprus, who was born here in 1454.

THE BOLLANI ERIZZO PALACE
PIETRO ARETINO LIVED HERE

The building is of the late 16th Century, probably the modernization of a pre-existent Byzantine or Gothic house.

373

CA' DA MOSTO

The building goes back to the 12th-13th Century, and though ruined by a heightening in the 17th Century shows clearly in its proportions the aspect of a Byzantine house-warehouse, with the ground floor arcade connecting with the interior warehouse for storage of goods, and the grouped central windows, and the single side windows of the first floor used as a dwelling.
It was the ancient dwelling of the famous navigator Alvise da Mosto who lived in the 15th Century.
From the 16th to the 18th Century the house became one of the most luxurious and renowned hotels of the city, with the sign of the « White Lion ».
Here lodged the Emperor Joseph II, and the Counts of the North, hereditary princes of Russia, for whom the Republic organized splendid and still famous festivals.

374

THE ANCIENT HOME OF THE NAVIGATOR ALVISE DA MOSTO
A LUXURIOUS HOTEL AT THE SIGN OF THE WHITE LION

THE PESARO PALACE
CONTAINS A GALLERY OF MODERN ART

On the area of three Gothic buildings Longhena raised one of the greatest palaces of the Grand Canal. The works began in 1676 and were interrupted in 1682 by the death of Longhena; they were taken up again only in 1710 by Antonio Gaspari who completed the building with the second floor following the original design of Longhena and built, to his own idea the lateral façade along the rio.
The building, one of the most important examples of Venetian Baroque civic architecture, houses the Museum of Modern Art; here are displayed Italian and foreign works of the 19th and 20th Centuries, with particular regard to Venetian art.

THE MANGILLI PALACE
THE ENGLISH AMBASSADOR
A. SMITH AND CANALETTO

The Ambassador Smith commissioned the architect Antonio Visentini to submit the plan of the building in the second half of the 18th Century.

THE MICHIEL DALLE COLONNE PALACE

So-called from the ground floor arcade which still shows its Byzantine origin despite successive reconstruction of the entire façade by Giuseppe Sardi in the second half of the 17th Century.

THE MICHIEL DAL BRUSÀ PALACE

So nicknamed because of the fire in 1774 which damaged gravely the ancient Gothic structure.
The restoration was carried out a few years later with the financial help of the Republic.

376

377

378

THE CA' D'ORO

One of the most lovely and significant civic buildings in Venice and one of the most conspicuous expressions of flamboyant Gothic.
In the first decades of the 15th Century (the structure was finished around 1434) Marino Contarini had this very splendid house built, known as « Golden » from the brilliant gilding and the polychromy of the façade, by Matteo Raverti with the aid of Lombard artisans and by the brothers Giovanni and Bartolomeo Bon.
While the structural elements of the portico recall those of Byzantine palaces, the two loggias of the upper floors represent the most elaborate expression of Venetian flamboyant Gothic.
The building now houses a Museum.

THE CHURCH OF SAN STAE
AND THE SCUOLA DEI BATTIORO

THE FONTANA PALACE
HERE C. REZZONICO,
LATER POPE CLEMENT XIII,
WAS BORN

The Fontanas were a rich family
of merchants from Piacenza, who,
once arrived in Venice, soon
formed part of the city nobility,
thanks also to very well-arranged
marriages.
The building, solemn and grandiose
presents clearly the normal scheme
of 16th Century palaces.

380

379

The church has very ancient origins.
Completely re-built in the second
half of the 17th Century, this
church, after a competition
announced by the Republic and won
by Domenico Rossi, was completed
with the new façade in the year 1709.
The Scuola at its side is a small
and dainty 18th Cent. building.

381

THE TRON PALACE
A CELEBRATED FESTIVITY IN
HONOUR OF JOSEPH II

THE BELLONI PALACE
A BUILDING BY LONGHENA

382

The Tron Palace was re-built
towards the end of the 16th Century
on classic lines in the place of a
pre-existing building.
The authority and wealth of the
Tron family allowed them in 1775
to organize a great festival in
honour of the Emperor.

The architect, Baldassare Longhena,
re-building an earlier Gothic edifice,
renewed this structure internally
and furnished it with a new façade
towards the middle of the
17th Century.
One might observe the
superabundance of the decorative
architectonic elements (balcony,
gables, etc.) emphasizing even on the
outside, the importance of the
main floor, according to Baroque
taste.

383

THE ERIZZO HOUSE
PAOLO ERIZZO DIED IN THE BATTLE IN 1469 AGAINST THE TURKS

THE MARCELLO PALACE
HERE THE COMPOSER BENEDETTO MARCELLO WAS BORN

384

After the Fontana palace a continuous series of façades interrupted only by the rio di Noale and farther by the rio della Maddalena characterizes this part of the right side of the Grand Canal.
The Gussoni Grimani della Vida Palace: building of the 16th Century possibly planned by the architect Sanmicheli. The frescoes, now almost completely disappeared, were executed by Tintoretto.
Barbarigo Palace: of the second half of the 16th Century, it, too, is decorated on the façade by frescoes by Camillo Ballini.

After the rio of the Maddalena, one after the other:
The Emo Palace of the 17th Century, the Soranzo Palace in Renaissance style, the plan of which is attributed to Sante Lombardo; the Molin Erizzo Palace, a Gothic building of the first half of the 15th Century. The great canvases of the main drawing room, still in place illustrate the heroic deeds of Paolo Erizzo, who died in 1469 fighting against the Turks.
Finally the Marcello Palace where in 1686 was born the celebrated composer, Benedetto Marcello.

385

FONDACO DEL MEGIO
FONDACO DEI TURCHI

Divided by a Canal, nearby stand the Warehouse of the Megio and the Warehouse of the Turks.
The former was built by the Republic in the 15th Century for use as a public granary.
The supplies of grain deposited here made it possible to face more serenely periods of famine, following periods of war, or bad harvests, and to control the price of flour and prevent speculations to the disadvantage of the people of Venice.
From the architectonic point of view the Warehouse of the Turks has no value to-day thanks to the destructive and wrong-headed restoration carried out in the 19th Century.
It would have been one of the most significant examples of great Byzantine house-warehouses.
It was, in fact built in the 13th Century by a very wealthy Pesaro merchant Giacomo Palmieri.
In 1381 it was acquired by the Marquis Nicolò V of Ferrara.
Such was the splendour of the building for size and decoration that often the Republic would let it out to entertain illustrious personages, such as, 1483, the Emperor of Constantinople, John Paleologus, in 1562, Alfonso d'Este and his wife, Eleanor.
In 1621 the Signoria rented it or acquired it from the Pesaro family, then the proprietors, to grant it to the Turkish community who maintained it until 1838 as a base for their commercial activities (warehouse, hotel, residence).

386

387

The Loredan family between the end of the 15th and the beginning of the 16th Century commissioned from Mauro Codussi the plan of the palace, which is one of the most significant examples of Venetian Renaissance architecture.
Robust yet at the same time elegant, the building is characterized above all by the typical large double-mullioned windows, a constant architectonic element invented by the architect Codussi. It seems that on the death of Codussi (1504) the works were brought to a finish by Lombardo.
On the right, looking on the garden, in the early years of the 17th Century, Vincenzo Scamozzi built a wing to enlarge the palace. It was, however, demolished by order of the Republic after the sentence of the then proprietors, the Grimani brothers, in 1658, for numerous and repeated criminal actions.
After the pardon which allowed them to return and recoup their fortunes, the Grimanis re-built that part of the Palace.
On the mezzanine floor lived and died on Feb. 13, 1883, Richard Wagner.

388

THE CHURCH OF SAN SIMEON PICCOLO

A GREEN DOME AT THE END OF THE GRAND CANAL

Built between 1718 and 1738 by the architect Giovanni Scalfarotto, who rebuilt it on Longhena lines in the assumption of the central plan and the dome, while in the porch preceded by a flight of stairs the adherence of the artist to the new neo-classic current seems clear.

389

388 The Grand Canal at the Railway Bridge
390 The Labia Palace and the church of San Geremia
391 The area round San Geremia and Cannaregio
392 The Cannaregio Canal
393 The bridge with the three arches

390

SAN GEREMIA

The foundation of the church of San Geremia goes back to the 11th Century. It took on its present aspect to the plan of Carlo Corbellini in the second half of the 18th Century.
Of the ancient structure remains the fine bell-tower in brickwork, most probably going back to the 13th Century.
On the left the Flangini Palace, architecture of the 18th Century by Giuseppe Sardi.

391

THE CANNAREGIO CANAL

THE BRIDGE WITH THE THREE ARCHES

The rio of Cannaregio, one of the widest canals in Venice, joins the Grand Canal to the western part of the lagoon towards the mainland of Mestre. It is crossed by two bridges: the first called delle Guglie from the obelisks adorning its parapets, was built in stone in 1580 to take the place of an earlier structure in wood; the second bridge, known as dei Tre Archi from the characteristic three arches forming it, is the work of the architect Tirali, carried out in 1688.

392

393

394

THE SESTIERE OF CANNAREGIO

395

The heavily populated sestiere di Cannaregio, characterized by its morphological conformation constituted by long, narrow islands separated by parallel canals and with a water-front, has its own particular fascination which distinguishes it clearly from other areas of the city. The greater part of these islands, above all the ones nearest the lagoon, were recovered in centuries of never-ceasing filling-in of shoals and sandbanks.
The building is Gothic, then Renaissance and Baroque. Logically there are no traces of anything older than the Byzantine period, since the area was not yet built upon.

THE CHARM OF THE FONDAMENTE ALONG THE PARALLEL RIOS OF SAN GIROLAMO, OF THE SENSA, OF THE MISERICORDIA, AND OF THE MADONNA DELL'ORTO.

A NETWORK OF CANALS WHICH FOLLOW THE NATURAL LINES OF THE ANCIENT BARENE BEFORE THE WORKS OF RECLAIMING AND BANKING UP.

396

The Strada Nuova (New Road) which leads from the Railway Station to the campo dei Santi Apostoli, and which runs longitudinally right through the sestiere di Cannaregio, is the result of a plan carried out in the year 1872 with the aim of giving a wide and easy way of getting to San Marco and Rialto, after the setting up of the new Railway Station at Santa Lucia. In order to arrive at this construction of a roadway the old existing houses were demolished over a wide area and numerous canals filled in.

THE LABIA PALACE AND G.B. TIEPOLO

A building of the mid-17th Century, possibly to the plan of the architect Alessandro Tremignon.
For this dwelling the Labia family, famous for their enormous wealth accumulated by commercial dealings and for having purchased with an astronomical sum of money their Venetian citizenship and nobility, spent equally conspicuous amounts both for the building of the imposing edifice and for the extremely elaborate decorations of the interior. To execute the frescoes of the rooms the most well-known and sought-after of the Venetian painters of the 18th Century Gian Battista Tiepolo was summoned. The artist, together with Mengozzi Colonna, who had worked out the architectonic perspectives, carried out this work between 1745 and 1750. They are episodes in the life of the Queen Cleopatra and figures of myth.

401

THE ANCIENT GHETTO

THE THREE SYNAGOGUES:
THE SCHOLA GRANDE OF THE GERMAN RITE
THE SCHOLA OF THE LEVANTINE RITE
THE SCHOLA OF THE SPANISH OR WESTERN RITE

402

403

In 1516, by permission of the Most Serene Republic, the Jews were all concentrated in a single area of the city, in the heart of the Cannaregio sestiere.
The increase of the population and the limits of the area at their disposition, compelled the Jews to build their houses very high; thus, they form to-day an evocative building background, slightly curved following the line of the canal at their back.
The denomination of « Ghetto » which was born in Venice and later on adopted universally to indicate the districts where Jews, and not only Jews, lived, derives from the existence in this locality of certain foundries where they « gettavano » (cast) mortars and cannons. From the word « gettare », that is « to cast », derived the words « getto » or « ghetto ». Such foundries existed from the 14th Century if not earlier, but had already ceased to exist by the 15th Century. From a document one also reads that the « ghetto » was enclosed all around by a wall and that « by means of a little door and a little bridge across a canal » one arrived in a district where the waste material from the furnaces used to accumulate. This second place, too, was called Ghetto, but with the addition of « Nuovo » (New) to distinguish it from the first, which then took the name of « Vecchio » (Old). And these denominations remain to-day to distinguish the two areas.
In the campiello della Scuola stand the synagogues, called Schole, each of which was officiated according to the rite of the country of origin of the Jews.
The Schola of the Western or Spanish rite was restored by Longhena in the first half of the 17th Century.

404

401 Campo del Ghetto Nuovo
402 Rio del Ghetto Nuovo
403, 404 Old houses on the Rio del Ghetto

THE CHURCH AND SCUOLA OF MISERICORDIA

THE ANCIENT ABBEY OF VAL VERDE

The complex comprises three very distinct buildings standing at the confluence of the Misericordia and Sensa rios with the canale di Noale; the Church, dedicated to St. Mary, has been several times re-built, and finally its façade was renewed in 1659 by Clemente Moli; the Scuola Vecchia (Old) is a Gothic building erected partly on the site of the convent of the old Abbey; the Scuola Nuova (New), one of the Great Scuole of Venice, was built starting from 1532 to the design of Jacopo Sansovino. The building of this last edifice, of enormous proportions, was continued over a number of years. The interior was finished in 1583; the exterior was never completed and, as can be seen to-day, remains with the bare brickwork structure.

405

CAMPO DEI MORI AND THE HOUSE OF THE CAMMELLO

407

Between the rios of the Sensa and that of the Madonna dell'Orto is the campo dei Mori, so-called because of three statues representing men of the Orient, on the Gothic house in the corner between the square and the water-front. At one time these three figures were said to be those of the three brothers, Rioba, Sandi and Alfani, rich merchants coming from Morea who established themselves in Venice to carry on their business. They adopted the name of Mastelli and under the same name is a Gothic palace looking on the canal in the rear, which bears on its façade a characteristic low relief of « a man leading a camel ».

Not far away, in fondamenta San Felice, the characteristic bridge giving access to a private house, the only example still in Venice without « bande » (parapets).

406

408

409

405 The Abbey and the Scuola della Misericordia
406 The Palace with the camel
407 The bridge without balustrades on Rio San Felice
408 Carving at the corner of the « Moor »
409 Campo dei Mori

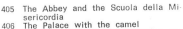

129

THE MADONNA DELL'ORTO
A FIFTEENTH CENTURY GOTHIC CHURCH

The church was built towards the middle of the 14th Century, by Fra' Tiberio of Parma and dedicated at first to St. Christopher.

It took on the title of Madonna dell'Orto after the transfer into the church of an ancient image of the Madonna that had come to light in a nearby garden. It was re-built at the beginning of the 15th Century. A characteristic element of the façade is provided by the series of niches, of Romanesque derivation, arranged as a crowning of the slopes of the lesser naves, with the statues of the twelve Apostles; as well as the two large lateral windows, in late Gothic style. The interior has three naves, no transept, and apsidal chapels.

Among the most interesting paintings, « St. John the Baptist and Saints », on the background of splendid landscape, by Cima da Conegliano; « Presentation of Mary at the Temple » by Jacopo Tintoretto, (on the outside of the doors of the ancient organ). Tintoretto belonged to the parish of the Madonna dell'Orto; he painted other important works for the church, and wished to be buried there. The campo, like that of the Misericordia, preserves the old-time brickwork paving, which gives to the place a most interesting and attractive sense of colour.

To the left of the church rises the bell-tower of the same era; to the right is the 15th Century cloister.

THE GESUITI
A CHURCH AND A MONASTERY OF AN ORDER EXPELLED FROM VENICE WITH CONTUMELY

The campo dei Gesuiti opens at the edge of the sestiere towards the northern part of the lagoon.
After the Convent stands the Church of Santa Maria dei Gesuiti, built to the plan of Domenico Rossi between the years 1714 and 1729. The façade is attributed to G. B. Fattoretto.
The Order of Jesuits bought the then-existing monastery from the ancient Order of the Crutched Friars when the latter was abolished by the Pope. The Scuola dei Crociferi, founded by the Doge Zeno in mid-13th Century, has on ceiling and walls a fine series of paintings by J. Palma the Y. representing episodes connected with the Order.
Inside the monumental Church of the Jesuits, one very large nave with lateral chapels, the decoration is very elaborate, with stuccoes, marbles and statues.
On an altar on the left is the altar piece representing « The Martyrdom of St. Laurence », a famous painting by Titian executed around 1558.

412

THE CHURCH OF
SANTA CATERINA
SAN FELICE
SANTA FOSCA

Along the water-front which goes from the campo dei Gesuiti, rises the ancient conventual complex of St. Catherine, with the Gothic church, de-consecrated, and unfortunately not open to the public, and the lovely cloister which still preserves the ogival arcades.
Going down the Strada Nuova, in the campo Santa Fosca stands the monument to Paolo Sarpi. The theological Counsellor of the Republic, was a strenuous defender of the city against Pope Paul V who, in the year 1606 had pronounced the interdict against Venice, the government of which had refused to bend to his will as regards ecclesiastical organization within its own State. Close to the nearby bridge of Santa Fosca the priest was attacked by hired assassins, but although he was wounded, he managed to escape death.
San Felice is a church built in 1531, possibly to the design of the architect Mauro Codussi.
In the campo Santi Apostoli stands the house of the Doge Marin Faliero, arcaded and with a fine Byzantine many-mullioned window on the façade.
According to tradition this was the dwelling place of Faliero before his election as Doge. The story is known of the plot which caused Marin Faliero, by then at an advanced age, to be sentenced to death by decapitation, which was put into execution publicly on April 16, 1355.

413

414

415

410 The church of Madonna dell'Orto
411 Rio Braso
412 The church of the Gesuiti, interior
413 Santa Caterina, cloister
414 The church of San Felice
415 The church of Santa Fosca

131

THE « REDENTORE » AND THE « SALUTE »

TWO TRADITIONAL ANNUAL FESTIVALS STILL OBSERVED TODAY, IN JULY AND NOVEMBER, TO COMMEMORATE THE END OF THE PLAGUES OF 1576 AND 1630.

The third Sunday of July is always dedicated to the feast of the Redentore, still extremely popular with the local people who flock to the island of the Giudecca, joined for the occasion to the quay of the Zattere by a bridge of boats.
In the evening the festivities continue on the water: a great number of boats gathers on the canals and the Venetians watch fireworks displays as they eat and drink.
By tradition the people then go to the Lido, to watch the sunrise from the beach.

The feast of the Salute, too, is a religious feast linked to the memory of the end of the plague. The Venetian people go in great numbers to beseech heaven's benevolence from the Virgin, so that mind and body may remain healthy. For the occasion a wooden bridge is built over boats between the two quays of the Grand Canal at the level of Campo Santa Maria del Giglio. The festival was at one time far greater, with the doge and nobility proceeding in pomp and circumstance for the religious observances and to give a stamp of officiality to the event.

THE BUCENTAUR AND THE MARRIAGE TO THE SEA

Ascension day was the festival of her very existence for Venice; the essence and meaning of her birth and power.
The marriage to the sea, celebrated symbolically at the entrance to the port at San Nicolò by the doge, who threw a golden ring into the sea from the Bucentaur, was the link uniting Venice with the Adriatic Sea, and a recognition of the fact that the city's major source of wealth and prosperity was indeed the sea: but is was at the same time an act of power or rather a public declaration of possession.
A great market-fair was held simultaneously in Piazza San Marco.

THE « REGATA »
FESTIVITIES FOR PEOPLE AND BOATS ALONG THE GRAND CANAL

The Grand Canal was the natural, spectacular « arena » for the « Regata », perfected and of increasingly widespread interest over the years, and increasingly spectacular as its official nature was emphasized. The actual regatta itself was preceded by a sumptuous parade of boats, magnificently decorated with rich trimmings and manned by numerous oarsmen. Like great carnival floats, these boats were ornamented at prow and stern with great allegorical and symbolic figures, generally with marine connotations. The doge himself, standing at the high prow of a large boat, travelled along the canal to receive the homage of the crowds gathered along the quaysides, in all the windows and on the roofs of the houses and palaces overlooking his route, or on the specially-constructed grandstands built on barges anchored alongside. The finishing point of the race was in front of Palazzo Foscari, where the doge himself awarded the prize, a suckling pig, to the winner. Although the « gondolino » for two rowers remained the classic boat for this type of regatta, other boats, divided as we would say into different classes, also raced before the main event, and the festival lasted all day and into the evening, dedicated to banquets and fireworks.

A race for « gondolini » with two rowers becomes the world-renowned « Regata » in Venice: a national festival celebrated over the centuries with great magnificence and pomp, but also with keen competition, by both the local population and foreigners.

Boats for one, five, twenty, fifty rowers, boats manned by women; all took turns at amusing the spectators who cheered now for one, now for another competitor. And as well as the official « Regata » that the government of the Republic fixed for September 14th, other regattas were organised, particularly prior to the 17th century, by the great Venetian families wishing thus to celebrate the election to the position of « Procuratore di San Marco » of one of their number. And then especially famous was the regatta held in honour of Crown Prince Frederick Christian of Poland in 1740, a great occasion when armies of painters, architects, set designers and decorators were employed for the furnishing and decorating of the boats, machines and palaces.

MASKS AND THE VENETIAN CARNIVAL

This is not the place to talk at length about the « Carnevale di Venezia », once renowned throughout Europe and still today famed as a historic event that reflected the customs of the day, commemorated in myriad paintings, etchings and descriptions.

Here we shall merely note that at that particular time Venice was permeated by a very singular feeling of animation shared by all, not only the nobility and the foreigners who flocked in droves to the lagoon city, but by the entire population, rich and poor. Participation was total; festivities and shows, although the most important were held in Piazza San Marco and the Piazzetta, were spread throughout all the districts of the city, in the squares and the « campielli » of Dorsoduro, Castello, Cannaregio and Santa Croce. First dances were organised in the open air, to the accompaniment of violins and 'cellos, or fifes and drums. These dances were often followed by dinners, with improvised tables lit by strings of small coloured balls containing candles. Dancing was permitted even in the squares near monasteries, but only until sunset. The use of the mask to disguise the wearer had been permitted during carnival time in Venice since the middle of the 13th century. The government made this concession as a result of a necessity, or rather specific request on the part of the citizens (in fact when attempts were made to limit or even prohibit the use of masks, the laws promulgated to this effect were completely ignored, despite the heavy penalties established). So strong was the need to be able to abandon themselves freely to the unrestrained merrymaking and the various amusements offered without fear of recognition during this brief period that the people's will overrode any law.

From the images that have come down to us, most of which date from the 18th century, we can get a very full idea of these great festive occasions, organised by the Republic itself with the aid of the « scuole » and tradesmen's associations, on Shrove Thursday and the last day of carnival: the grandstands and rows of seats built especially for the hordes of tumultuous spectators, the processions of masks dancing, singing and making music, and the shows and exhibitions themselves: the above-mentioned bull-chase, the acrobatics of the Turk on the double rope stretched between the top of the Campanile and the loggia of the Ducal Palace; the « Herculean » demonstrations of strength, repeated on other days in the squares or on boats in the wider canals, the fireworks set off from fabulously constructed towers. The doge and nobility were present in force in their most sumptuous robes.

BULL
AND BEAR
BAITING

Bull baiting in Venice has very ancient origins, and although many condemned it severely as too inhuman, it was always tollerated and even encouraged and promoted by the government of the Republic itself. The event was held each year at carnival time all during the long centuries of the Republic (it was prohibited by law only in 1802) in the largest squares of the city, the islands and the mainland. And on special occasions even in Piazza San Marco.

The bull was chased around and enraged in every possible way (pushed, held down, beaten, turned over) and sometimes had fireworks tied to its horns. In the end its head was cut off in a single stroke with heavy two-handed swords, and butchered. The baiting always took place between the bull and dogs, specially trained to worry the unfortunate animal, and in particular to bite its ears.

There were however two kinds of bull baiting. In one, the bull's horns were tied with one or two ropes held by strong men who thus kept it prisoner and by sudden pulls and tugs or letting go, attempted to help the bull escape the attacking dogs (which bit only at its ears) and at the same time incited it to retaliate. When a dog managed to attach itself to the bull's ears, a « cavacane », dog remover, ran to detach it again. The other kind of baiting was « a toro molai », i. e. the bull was loose, not held by ropes, but with the same system of dogs and « cavacane ».

Sometimes bear baiting was incorporated into the bull baiting. Here the animal was tied to a pole by a chain and heavy collar that allowed it a few yards of movements. The dogs were on long leashes manoeuvred by expert handlers and set on the bear, which defended itself as best it could. When it managed to bite a dog, a « cavaorsi » bear-remover, used wooden sticks poked into its mouth to force it to free its prey.

KILL THE CAT
WITH SHAVED HEAD

CATCH THE DUCK
IN THE WATER

A cruel custom permitted the tying of a cat to a table by its body, leaving head and paws free.
Those playing this « game » had to strike the animal, only with their completely shaved heads, until they killed it. The consequences may easily be imagined.
Another rather less cruel game was that of tying a goose by its feet across a canal near a bridge. The competitors jumped from the bridge so as to catch the animal by the neck and plunge into the water, the trophy firmly clutched in their hands.
The « cuccagna » was also played: a duck was placed at the top of a tall greased pole.
During carnival time different kinds of shows and entertainment were put on, such as « kill the with shaved head ».

THE PLAYERS'
STAGE

THE MARIONETTE
THEATRE

Carnival time in Venice was one of the most lively and spectacular periods of the year, for both nobles and commoners, and for foreign visitors to the city, and it was justly famous throughout Europe.
During these times the Piazza, the Piazzetta and the squares of the city were full of little cabins and stages where singers, actors, jugglers and puppet showmen provided a constant stream of entertainment to delight spectators of all ages and tastes.
In Piazza San Marco the singers and actors performed on wooden stages with painted scenery behind them and amused an audience that was always quite numerous. These performers also gave private productions in the houses and gardens of noble Venetians.
But it was above all in the streets and public buildings such as theatres and concert halls that most events took place during the carnival festivities.

VENETIAN CHURCHES IN EXISTENCE OR DEMOLISHED

Sant'AGNESE (St. Agnes) *(closed)*
Sant'AGOSTIN (St. Augustine) *(demolished)*
Sant'ALVISE
Sant'ANDREA (St. Andrew) della Zirada *(closed)*
Sant'ANGELO (St. Angel) *(demolished)*
ANGELO RAFFAELE (The Angel Raphael)
Sant'ANNA *(closed)*
Sant'ANTONIN (Antony)
Sant'ANTONIO (Antony) *(demolished)*
Sant'APOLLONIA (cloister)
Sant'APONAL *(closed)*
Santi APOSTOLI (Holy Apostles)
ASCENSIONE (Ascension) *(demolished)*
San BARNABA
San BASEGIO *(demolished)*
San BASSO *(closed)*
San BENETTO *(closed)*
San BIAGIO (Blaise) *(closed)*
San BIAGIO e CATALDO *(demolished)*
San BOLDO *(demolished)*
San BONAVENTURA (Bonaventure) *(closed)*
San BORTOLOMIO (Bartholomew)
Ca' di DIO (House of God) *(closed)*
San CANCIANO
CAPPUCCINE *(closed)*
CARITÀ (Charity) *(closed)*
CARMINI
San CASSIANO (Cassian)
CATECUMENI (Catechumens) *(closed)*
Santa CATERINA *(closed)*
CELESTIA *(demolished)*
Santa CHIARA (Clara) *(demolished)*
CONVERTITE *(closed)*
CORPUS DOMINI *(demolished)*
Santi COSMA e DAMIANO (Cosmas and Damian) *(demolished)*

CROCE (Cross) *(closed)*
San DANIELE *(demolished)*
San DOMENICO (St. Dominic) *(demolished)*
Sant'ELENA
EREMITE (Hermits) *(closed)*
Sant'EUFEMIA
San FANTIN
FAVA
San FELICE (Felix)
Santi FILIPPO e GIACOMO (Philip and James) *(demolished)*
Santa FOSCA
San FRANCESCO di PAOLA
San FRANCESCO della VIGNA
FRARI (Friars)
San GALLO (Gall) *(closed)*
San GEMINIANO *(demolished)*
San GEREMIA (Jeremiah)
GESUATI
GESUITI (Jesuits)
GESÙ e MARIA (Jesus and Mary) *(demolished)*
San GIACOMETTO
San GIACOMO (James) *(demolished)*
San GIACOMO dell'ORIO
San GIOACCHINO (Joachim) *(closed)*
San GIOBBE (Job)
San GIORGIO dei GRECI *(closed)*
San GIORGIO MAGGIORE
San GIOVANNI BATTISTA (St. John the Baptist) *(demolished)*
San GIOVANNI in BRAGORA
San GIOVANNI ELEMOSINARIO (St. John the Almsgiver)
San GIOVANNI EVANGELISTA *(closed)*
San GIOVANNI CRISOSTOMO (St. John Chrysostom)
San GIOVANNI LATERANO *(demolished)*
San GIOVANNI di MALTA *(closed)*
San GIOVANNI NOVO (New) *(closed)*

San GIOVANNI e PAOLO
San GIROLAMO (Jerome) *(closed)*
San GIUSEPPE (Joseph)
Santa GIUSTINA *(closed)*
San GREGORIO (Gregory) *(closed)*
San LEONARDO *(closed)*
San LIO
San LORENZO (Laurence) *(closed)*
San LUCA (Luke)
Santa LUCIA (Lucy)
MADDALENA (Magdalene) *(closed)*
MADONNA dell'ARSENALE *(demolished)*
MADONNA dell'ORTO
San MARCO
San MARCUOLA
Santa MARGHERITA *(closed)*
Santa MARIA FORMOSA
Santa MARIA del GIGLIO (St. Mary of the Lily)
Santa MARIA MAGGIORE *(closed)*
Santa MARIA MATER DOMINI (St. Mary Mother of God)
Santa MARIA NOVA *(demolished)*
Santa MARIA del PIANTO (St. Mary the Mourner)
Santa MARIA della VISITAZIONE *(closed)*
Santa MARINA *(demolished)*
Santa MARTA *(closed)*
San MARTINO
San MARZIALE (Martial)
San MAURIZIO (Maurice)
MENDICANTI (Mendicants) *(closed)*
MIRACOLI (Miracles)
MISERICORDIA (Mercy) *(closed)*
San MOISÉ (Moses)
San NICOLETTO della LATTUGA *(demolished)*
San NICOLÒ di BARI *(demolished)*
San NICOLÒ dei MENDICOLI NOME DI GESÙ (Name of Jesus)
OGNISSANTI (All Saints) *(closed)*
OSPEDALETTO (Hospital) *(closed)*
San PANTALON (Pantaleon)
San PATERNIAN (Paterine) *(demolished)*
PENITENTI (Penitents) *(closed)*
PIETÀ (Compassion)
San PIETRO di CASTELLO
San PAOLO
San PROVOLO *(demolished)*
REDENTORE (Redeemer)
San ROCCO (Rock) *(closed)*
SALUTE (Health)
San SALVADOR (Saviour)
SCALZI (Discalced)
San SEBASTIANO (Sebastian)
San SEPOLCRO (Holy Sepulchre) *(demolished)*
San SEVERO (Severus) *(demolished)*
San SIMEON GRANDE
San SIMEON PICCOLO *(closed)*
SOCCORSO (Aid) *(closed)*
Santa SOFIA
SPIRITO SANTO (Holy Spirit) *(demolished)*
San STAE *(closed)*
Santo STEFANO (Stephen)
San STIN *(demolished)*
Terese (Teresa) *(closed)*
Santa TERNITA *(demolished)*
TOLENTINI
San TOMÀ (Thomas) *(closed)*
TRINITÀ (Trinity) *(demolished)*
San TROVASO
UMILTÀ (Humility) *(demolished)*
VERGINI *(demolished)*
San VIDAL *(closed)*
San VIO *(demolished)*
San ZACCARIA (Zachary)
San ZAN DEGOLÀ *(closed)*
ZITELLE (Spinsters) *(closed)*

THE ISLANDS
IN THE LAGOON

AMMIANA *(disappeared)*
Sant'ANDREA della CERTOSA

416

BURANO
San CLEMENTE
COSTANZIACA *(disappeared)*
San CRISTOFORO della PACE (St. Christopher of Peace) *(cemetery)*
Sant'ERASMO (St. Erasmus)
San FRANCESCO del DESERTO (St. Francis of the Desert)
San GIACOMO in PALUO (St. James in the Marsh)
San GIORGIO
San GIORGIO in ALGA
GIUDECCA
LAZZARETTO VECCHIO
San LAZZARO degli ARMENI (St. Lazarus of the Armenians)
LIDO
MALAMOCCO
San MARCO in BOCCA LAMA
Santa MARIA delle GRAZIE (St. Mary of Grace)
MAZZORBO
San MICHELE *(cemetery)*
MURANO
PELLESTRINA

San PIETRO in VOLTA
PORTO SECCO
POVEGLIA
SACCA SESSOLA
San SERVOLO
Santo SPIRITO
TORCELLO
VIGNOLE

417

418

THE DOGES

Paolo Lucio Anafesto	697	Andrea Contarini	1368
Marcello Tegalliano	717	Michele Morosini	1382
Orso Ipato	726	Antonio Venier	1382
Teodato Ipato	742	Michele Steno	1400
Galla Gaulo	755	Tommaso Mocenigo	1414
Domenico Monegario	756	Francesco Foscari	1423
Maurizio Galbaio	764	Pasquale Malipiero	1457
Giovanni Galbaio	787	Cristoforo Moro	1462
Obelerio Antenoreo	804	Nicolò Tron	1471
The seat of government was transferred from Malamocco to Rivoalto		Nicolò Marcello	1473
		Pietro Mocenigo	1474
Angelo Partecipazio	811	Andrea Vendramin	1476
Giustiniano Partecipazio	827	Giovanni Mocenigo	1478
Giovanni I Partecipazio	829	Marco Barbarigo	1485
Pietro Tradonico	836	Agostino Barbarigo	1486
Orso I Partecipazio	864	Leonardo Loredan	1501
Giovanni II Partecipazio	881	Antonio Grimani	1521
Pietro I Candiano	887	Andrea Gritti	1523
Pietro Tribuno	888	Pietro Lando	1539
Orso II Partecipazio	912	Francesco Donà	1545
Pietro II Candiano	932	Marcantonio Trevisan	1553
Pietro Partecipazio	939	Francesco Venier	1554
Pietro III Candiano	942	Lorenzo Priuli	1556
Pietro IV Candiano	959	Girolamo Priuli	1559
Pietro I Orseolo	976	Pietro Loredan	1567
Vitale Candiano	978	Alvise I Mocenigo	1570
Tribuno Memmo	979	Sebastiano Venier	1577
Pietro II Orseolo	991	Nicolò da Ponte	1578
Ottone Orseolo	1008	Pasquale Cicogna	1585
Pietro Centranico	1026	Marino Grimani	1595
Domenico Flabanico	1032	Lenoardo Donà	1606
Domenico Contarini	1043	Marcantonio Memmo	1612
Domenico Selvo	1071	Giovanni Bembo	1615
Vitale Falier	1084	Nicolò Donà	1618
Vitale I Michiel	1096	Antonio Priuli	1618
Ordelafo Falier	1102	Francesco Contarini	1623
Domenico Michiel	1118	Giovanni Cornaro	1625
Pietro Polani	1130	Nicolò Contarini	1630
Domenico Morosini	1148	Francesco Erizzo	1631
Vitale II Michiel	1156	Francesco Molin	1646
Sebastiano Ziani	1172	Carlo Contarini	1655
Orio Malipiero	1178	Francesco Corner	1656
Enrico Dandolo	1192	Bertuccio Valier	1656
Pietro Ziani	1205	Giovanni Pesaro	1658
Jacopo Tiepolo	1229	Domenico Contarini	1659
Marino Morosini	1249	Nicolò Sagredo	1675
Reniero Zeno	1253	Luigi Contarini	1676
Lorenzo Tiepolo	1268	Marcantonio Giustinian	1684
Jacopo Contarini	1275	Francesco Morosini	1688
Giovanni Dandolo	1280	Silvestro Valier	1694
Pietro Gradenigo	1296	Alvise II Mocenigo	1700
Marino Zorzi	1311	Giovanni II Corner	1709
Giovanni Soranzo	1312	Alvise III Mocenigo	1722
Francesco Dandolo	1329	Carlo Ruzzini	1732
Bartolomeo Gradenigo	1339	Alvise Pisani	1735
Andrea Dandolo	1343	Pietro Grimani	1741
Marino Faliero	1354	Francesco Loredan	1752
Giovanni Gradenigo	1355	Marco Foscarini	1762
Giovanni Dolfin	1356	Alvise IV Mocenigo	1763
Lorenzo Celsi	1361	Paolo Renier	1779
Marco Corner	1365	Lodovico Manin	1789

416 « The life of St. Ursula », V. Carpaccio (Academy)
417 « A saint's head », mosaic (Marciana Museum)
418 « David », mosaic (Basilica of St. Mark)

141

INDEX OF THE GREATEST ARTISTS WHO WORKED IN VENICE

ALBANESI
ANGELO CUSTODE
BARBIERI (Barbers)
BARCAROLI (Boatmen)
BATTILORO (Gold-Beaters)
BATTUTI (Flagellants)
BOMBARDIERI (Munition-Makers)
BUONA MORTE
CALAFATI (Caulkers)
CALEGHERI (Shoemakers)
CARITÀ (Charity)
CARMINI
CASSELLERI (Cabinet-Makers)
CRISTO
FRUTTAROLI (Greengrocers)
GARBELADORI (Riddlers)
GARZOTTI (Carders)
GRECI (Greeks)
LANERI (Woollen-Drapers)
LINAROLI (Flax-Dressers)
LUGANEGHERI (Sausage-Makers)
MERCANTI (Merchants)
MERCANTI DI VINO (Wine Dealers)
MERCIAI (Haberdashers)
MISERICORDIA
MURERI (Masons)
NOBILI (Nobles)
OREFICI (Goldsmiths)
PASSIONE (Passion)
PICAI
PISTORI (Bakers)
Pittori (Painters)
POLLAIUOLI (Poulterers)
PURIFICAZIONE (Purification)
SARTORI (Tailors)
SCHIAVONI (Dalmatians)
SETAIOLI (Silk-Workers)
SOTTI
SPIRITO SANTO
TAJAPIERA (Stone-Cutters)
TESSITORI DI SETA (Silk-Weavers)
TRINITÀ
VAROTARI (Furriers)
SCUOLE GRANDI
SAN GIOVANNI EVANGELISTA
SAN MARCO
SANTA MARIA DELLA CARITÀ
SANTA MARIA DELLA MISERICORDIA
SAN ROCCO
SAN TEODORO

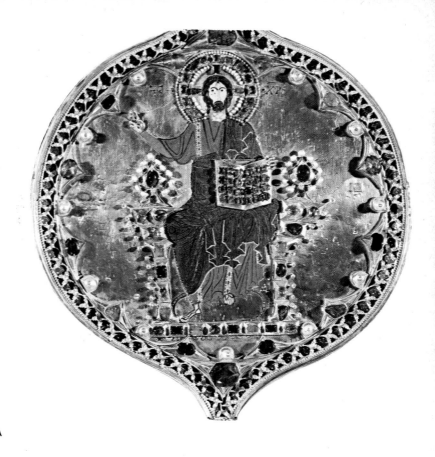

ARCHITECTS, SCULPTORS, PAINTERS, DECORATORS, ARMOURERS, CERAMIC ARTISTS, ENGRAVERS, MOSAIC ARTISTS.

Title:
Venice and its treasures

Layout:
Edizioni Storti - Venezia

Photos:
Ballarin, Storti - Venezia
Tappeiner - Merano

Printers:
Lito Terrazzi - Firenze

Printed for:
Ditta Giuseppe Gerlin
San Marco, S. Angelo 3572/a
Venezia. Tel. (041) 709.476

GENERAL INDEX

422